Portraits
of the
Pecos Frontier

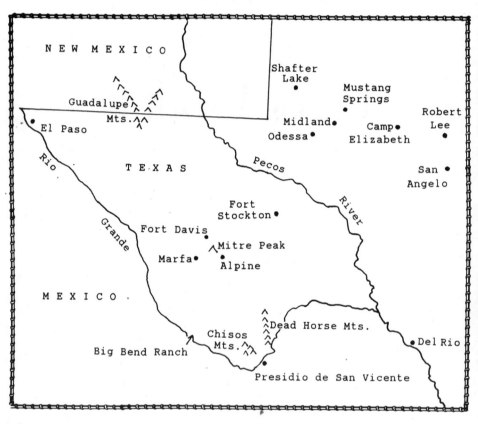

Map of the Pecos country.

Portraits of the Pecos Frontier

By Patrick Dearen

Texas Tech University Press

To Bambi and Wesley, my best friends

This book was set in ITC Caslon and printed on acid-free paper that meets the guidelines for permanence and durability of the Committee on Production Guidelines for Book Longevity of the Council on Library Resources. ∞

Cover design by Kerri Carter
Cover photo by Chad Puerling

Manufactured in the United States of America

Library of Congress Cataloging-in-Publication Data

Dearen, Patrick.
    Portraits of the Pecos frontier / by Patrick Dearen.
        p. cm.
    Includes bibliographical references and index.
    ISBN 0–89672–288–0 (pbk.)
    1. Trans-Pecos (N.M. and Tex.)—History. I. Title.
F802.P3D43 1993   92–29829
976.4′ 9—dc20   CIP

Texas Tech University Press
Lubbock, Texas 79409-1037 USA

93 94 95 96 97 98 99 00 01 / 9 8 7 6 5 4 3 2 1

Contents

❧

Foreword

✿

*T*he Pecos country of which Patrick Dearen writes would be—by nearly anyone's definition—largely a desert. It is huge, dry, and, to the eyes of most strangers, barren and forbidding. Yet, it has a tendency to grow on people who remain long enough to discover its hidden beauties, to find the infinite variety of life in what seems at first to be emptiness, and to be intrigued by mysteries whose answers remain always just beyond our fingertips.

Bill Allman, the cable tool driller to whom Dearen devotes a segment of the book, came to West Texas as a young man seeking work in early oil boom days and thought it the most desolate place he had ever seen. Nevertheless, he grew to love it and gave it the remainder of a long lifetime. Ardeth Allman, his helpmate for some sixty or so years, once related how her mother came down from Kansas to visit and was so horrified by the raw environment that she almost dragged her newly married daughter away against her will. The Allmans stayed to become much-beloved community leaders in Crane, typical of the Permian Basin oil towns.

For those born, as I was, in what Dearen calls the Pecos frontier, the uniqueness of this region is accepted and embraced. What outsiders regard as strange, we take as perfectly natural. However far we may eventually wander, it remains always our *querencia*, the home of our hearts.

Why? Partly the reason has to be the land itself: the broad greasewood flats and their pleasant seasonal scent carried to us on the strong north wind; the constantly moving sandhills that shimmer golden in the sun and occasionally yield a long-buried secret of a time we can only speculate upon; the Pecos River bordered by low salt cedars; the Concho River lined with tall pecan trees; the

Rio Grande of many moods, flowing languidly across long stretches of desert, turning to sudden violence as it courses through the narrow passageways between towering canyon walls, then quieting again for the remainder of its long, snake-track journey until its waters merge into those of the Gulf.

And there are the western mountains: the Guadalupes, the Davis, and the Chisos of the Big Bend, standing blue and deceptively cool as one stares longingly toward them across the vastness of the sunbaked flatlands. It is a country of contrasts and contradictions, illusions and stark realities.

Yet, there is much more to it than the land. In any country, one remembers most its people. There is something about the Pecos frontier—from San Angelo west to the mountains—that marks those who make their homes there. That mark is not always easy to define. Like other mysteries of the land, its identity remains just beyond our fingertips, but we sense that it is there. Despite increasing urbanization and amalgamation of Americans into a cookie-cutter sameness from sea to sea, individuality remains strong in the West Texas genes.

Perhaps it is that this land has been and remains a constant challenge to those who live upon it. Compared to that in areas east of us, life in West Texas has never been easy. Its fruits are not gathered without sweat, tears, and occasionally a little blood. Seldom is there enough rain. Those who live from the land—the ranchers and farmers—feel this pressure the most, but even in the cities, West Texans remain aware that theirs is a land where the next drought is likely to begin tomorrow if not today, and water must be measured and guarded like the treasure that it is.

People of the Pecos frontier have been shaped, too, by their history and their legends. Often it is difficult to separate one from the other, for much of what happened in earlier times has passed into folklore, and there are many versions from which to choose the one that appeals most to the individual sense of logic, of romance, of mystery.

This was home first to the Indians, from Midland Man to the Jumanos who gathered salt in wicker baskets from the dust-coated saline crust of Juan Cordona Lake, to the Apaches and the Comanches who fought and bloodied one another over it until the white man wrested it from both with his numbers and overwhelming firepower. The Spaniards came in search of mineral wealth, but left little behind except shadowy legends of slavery and lost treasures that still haunt certain remote and mystic places. Where the Spaniards sought gold and silver, hoping to rob the land and then leave it, the Mexicans came to stay, tilling the rare arable places and tending their herds and flocks. And last came the English-speaking people from the east to found their large ranches, to build their towns and their railroads and, finally, to drill deep into the earth for a treasure greater than the Spaniards ever dreamed.

Dearen has devoted much of his life to researching the Pecos frontier, its environmental as well as its human history, its wealth of folklore from which only a little has been recorded on paper. Some he has obtained by researching books and old records, as in his tracing of prehistoric inhabitants and Jeff Davis's camels. Some has come from interviews with people who have experienced West Texas in their own individual ways, from the cowboy to the driller, to the chasers of ghosts and ghost lights. Some he has experienced in a most personal way, through his own strenuous outings into the mountains and canyons of the Guadalupes and the Big Bend, through riding in the engine of a freight train across the Permian Basin, from sitting in a hobo jungle and hopping a freight with the transients who follow the rails from one such jungle to another.

He has ridden with the Border Patrol in its pursuit of illegal aliens, "wetbacks" in West Texas parlance. And he has listened sympathetically to aliens still at large—*mojados* who have managed to escape the patrolmen but live in the shadows, fearing the day they may confront the *migra* and be deported back to Mexico and its dead-end poverty. He tells their story with compassion, though he understands as well the sad necessity of those deportations lest the country be overwhelmed by a tide of illegal immigration.

And he understands—if any of us can truly understand—the emotions and motivations of the tragic Charles Ray "Cowboy" Walls, born a hundred years out of his natural time and finding himself a forlorn misfit in his own country. The author traces as well as anybody can—for only Walls knew for sure where and how he traveled—his brief, doomed flight from the twentieth century.

Using the drama and color of a gifted storyteller—a contemporary J. Frank Dobie—Patrick Dearen in these pages lets us sample the many flavors of his Pecos frontier. There are still thousands more stories to be told out of this special corner of our country. Let us hope he will continue telling them, for they cry out to be told.

Elmer Kelton

Preface

❀

We struggled one blazing June afternoon up a primitive trail in the Guadalupe Mountains, my father and I, on the baptismal backpack trek for either of us. Our appreciation for the rugged beauty about us was dulled somewhat by the rigors of the climb, which brought lungs heaving like bellows and left aching muscles and saddle-sore shoulders. Three hours and twenty-five minutes and a vertical half-mile later, we burst upon the summit of the range and of Texas to be swallowed by a ponderosa pine forest, where we sought shelter in our nylon tent from raging winds that night. As day broke over this wilderness the next morning, ushering in my father's sixty-third birthday, we stood on rimrock sentineling Pine Canyon below, the mighty apex of Guadalupe Peak to the south, and one hundred miles of mountain and desert country unfurling to the southeast like an angry ocean.

Though I was a native West Texan, it was not until then that I realized the Pecos River country truly is a place that defies absolute description. An artist's brush might make a stroke here, a dab there, but how could it ever paint a picture of a vast land of contrasts in its entirety?

Later, as a writer seeking to capture the region with words, I realized I faced the same problem as an artist who, if commissioned to paint the Pecos country, would find it an impossible task. I thought back to years of travel through the area, of hundreds of West Texans with whom I had shared and laughed, of meaningful days of self-discovery in the backcountry, and I knew the overall picture was too varied and emotional for one person—artist *or* writer—ever to capture fully. And so, like that artist who can only find and commit to canvas an image here, an image there, I set out

to paint with words the Pecos country I know, through portraits of intriguing individuals and their folklore, forgotten sites and their legends, and hidden places that still kindle a primeval fire inside man. I hoped that a reader, by taking the portraits as a whole, would gain a glimpse into the essence of the Pecos country, as well as acquire a feel for the people who have been shaped by the land or who have been forced by circumstance to live and die there.

In chasing those portraits I traveled thousands of miles in crisscrossing that still-frontier lying between San Angelo on the east and El Paso on the west, a region dwarfing many states yet coursed by but one significant waterway, the Pecos River itself. I drove by conventional pickup where I could, and when the roads got too rough—or nonexistent—I took to four-wheel drive and, finally, mere hiking boots.

I climbed high into the Chisos range and searched for evidence of a legendary lost mine. Equally legendary "ghost lights" teased me across an arid plain when I hunted them on a dark night. I dared the spirits by staying in a supposed haunted house in the Davis Mountains and listened in awe to nocturnal sounds like the creaking of coffin lids. I walked the tracks of dinosaurs long-dead and studied Indian signs at a spring and cavalry signs at a forgotten army camp. I endured days of solitude in the Guadalupe back-country, slithered through the mud of a cavern sparkling with fossils, struggled hand-over-hand up a Davis Mountains peak.

I heard tales spun by adventurers and seekers and challenged many of the same wilderness spots: the Rio Grande rapids, Big Bend desert, Coke County canyons. I huddled in the mud of a bluff overlooking the Rio Grande and desolation of Mexico and

---

The Pecos frontier as seen from the upper slope of Mitre Peak in the Davis Mountains. (Courtesy Chad Puerling)

watched illegal aliens and border patrolmen play a game that meant life or death. I donned old clothes and assumed the role of a tramp in the freight yards to discover the modern-day hobo as he really is. I smelled the burnt flesh at roundups and listened spellbound to tales of the early-day oil patch.

What I found in that several-year odyssey was a diversity that astounded even this native West Texan.

When the last portrait finally had been committed to paper and to heart, I felt bonded to the land with as much surety as awe-inspiring sunsets to Castle Gap, the longhorn to the cattle trails of the Pecos, the mesquite and creosote to the wind-blown flats.

Now saddle up, tighten the cinches, and get ready for a bucking bronc ride through the greatness that is the Pecos frontier.

Part 1

Mysteries

The Lost Chisos Mine

*I*n the vastness of the range called Chisos lurks a secret.

Two centuries old, it lies buried, perhaps, beneath untold tons of sheer rock, concealed for the ages. It is the mystery of the Lost Chisos Mine, held captive in legend somewhere in that craggy island range which juts from the Chihuahuan Desert to sentinel the Big Bend desolation of West Texas and the equally imposing wilderness of Mexico. In three directions, beyond the thin veil of greenery marking the Rio Grande, hazy, barren mountains jag the horizon in another country, while to the north, stretches a searing desert flat broken by deeply chiseled drainages and gnarled crags. To the Spanish *conquistadores* it was the *Despoblado*—the uninhabited land. The explorers sent by Spain faded into history long ago, yet the land remains largely tenantless, one still untamed, still laden with mystique, and still, perhaps, replete with lost riches.

Guardian of the Chisos range, contained in its entirety within present-day Big Bend National Park, is Emory Peak, which crests at 7,835 feet—a full 6,000 feet above the Rio Grande less than twenty air miles to the south and southeast. The mountain, crowned by a fist of rock, and the lesser peaks kneeling before it, first were noted landmarks to early Indians and, by the latter eighteenth century, to Spaniards seeking dominion over the *Despoblado*. Even at that early date, the range already had gained its name. "I have . . . discovered that Zapato Tuerto [an Apache chief] was attacked in the Chisos and not in the Sierra del Carmen," reported Don Juan Bautista Elguezabel to Jacobo Ugarte at Presidio del Norte, April 21, 1787.

By the mid-nineteenth century, American explorers, as well, had taken note of the Chisos. Marine T. W. Chandler, conducting a topographic survey of the Big Bend in 1852 for the United States and Mexican Boundary Commission, described the range:

> . . . From its peculiar shape and great height, [one peak] was long and anxiously watched during the progress of our survey. From many places on the line it was taken as a prominent point on which to direct the instrument; and, though the face of the country might change during our progress down the river [Rio Grande], still, unmistakable and unchangeable, far above the surrounding mountains, this peak reared its well known head. The windings of the river, and the progress of our survey, led us gradually nearer to this point of interest, and it was found to be a part of a cluster, rather than range, of mountains on the American side, known as "Los Chisos." For this peak . . . we have proposed the name of Mount Emory.

The range continued to mesmerize all who saw it loom jagged against the sky throughout the nineteenth century. "Nowhere have I found such a wildly weird country," wrote U.S. Treasury agent William Ferguson in the *San Antonio Express* in 1896:

> . . . Emotions are stirred by the grandeur and beauty of the scenery and the ever-changing play of light and shadows. Never have I beheld such a display of glory as falls at sunset on the bald head of the Chisos Mountains, as witnessed at a distance of twenty-five miles. No painter could mix colors to justly portray it. No words can describe its splendour. First orange, then pink, then crimson, and last of all darkening purple, threw tints on the mountain's dark background and all faded insensible into neutral twilight.

Robert T. Hill, challenging the Rio Grande canyons by wooden boat as part of an 1899 United States Geological Survey expedition, was no less impressed with the Chisos: "They are ragged points of a reddish granitic rock, weathering into yellow and orange colors like those from which the Yellowstone derives its name: they rise almost straight into the air. . . . The vertical slopes of the peaks, rifted here and there by joints and seams, give to them the aspect of being clad in filmy drapery."

While some researchers believe the term "Chisos" is the plural form of an Apache tribal name—*Chis-sah* or *Chishi* ("People of the Forest")—by the time of Hill's expedition the word already long had been associated with the supernatural by those of Mexican Indian descent who lived in the range's shadow. They believed it either a corruption of the Spanish word *hechizo*—"bewitched"—or an Indian word meaning "ghosts." It was the latter meaning Hill applied to it in 1899, equating the name with the range's appearance:

> The crowning feature of this desert is the lofty and peculiar group of peaks known as Los Chisos ("the ghosts"). These weird forms are appropriately named.... Wherever one climbs out of the low stream grove [of the Rio Grande] these peaks stare him in the face like a group of white-clad spirits rising from a base of misty gray shadow and vegetation. Many are the weird forms and outlines which the peaks assume.

Originally, however, the Chisos may have become associated with ghosts for quite a different reason than mere physical appearance—and that reason is intrinsically enmeshed in the story of the Lost Chisos Mine. That vanished hoard lies in the realm of unsubstantiated legend, though one built on the documented facts of Spanish attempts to control the *Despoblado*, as well as their ever-present "Coronado complex"—the obsession to find gold or silver in the New World.

Dominion over a land such as the Big Bend was not something to be essayed without forethought, not when it held such inhospitable deserts and impenetrable mountains—all arid in the extreme and subject not only to the searing sun but to all manner of poisonous snakes and scorpions. Equally threatening were the Apache warmongers who, unlike the hundred thousand peaceful Indians who farmed along the Rio Grande from present-day El Paso to Presidio, greeted the intrusion of outsiders into their kingdom with a war cry and *shoosh* of arrow.

Realizing the terrain rendered infeasible any large-scale attempt to rid the *Despoblado* of Apaches, who held a close kinship with the desert, Governor Antonio de Oca Sarmiento of Nueva Vizcaya proposed in 1667 that a line of "watchtowers," or presidios, be set up at assailable points. He recommended they be positioned at regular intervals to allow mutual support, and each be manned by ten soldiers and four peaceful Indians. Sarmiento's plan went largely ignored for generations, and by 1728 the Indian threat had worsened.

With the acquisition of the horse, Comanches had migrated southward into Apacheria and become the most feared warriors ever known to North America. Finally, with Comanche and Apache raids becoming commonplace in New Spain's northern reaches in the 1770s, officials implemented Sarmiento's presidio plan. With it, not only did they seek to control tribes which glorified warfare, they also furthered their efforts to proselytize friendly Indians along the Rio Grande—a factor which led to the construction of missions at the presidios.

One of the two major prongs of the Comanche War Trail crossed the Rio Grande just upstream of mighty Mariscal Canyon. A couple of hours' ride downriver, beyond the lesser gorge now called San Vicente Canyon, lay a more ancient Indian ford in proximity to tillable land, considerations which prompted Hugo Oconor in April 1773 to select a nearby knoll on the southeast side of the Rio Grande for construction of a presidio. Lying 1,920 feet above sea level and situated approximately nineteen air miles southeast of Emory Peak, it would be known as Presidio de San Vicente, named in honor of Saint Vincent, the mission's patron saint.

The ruins of Presidio de San Vicente. (Archives of the Big Bend, Sul Ross State University; Alpine, Texas; photograph by Glenn Burgess)

Ordering the garrison at the presidio of San Saba in present-day Menard County transferred to San Vicente, Oconor returned in 1774 to find construction lagging behind schedule. Within a short while, however, the outpost—constructed of adobe brick and timbers—stood sentinel over the *Despoblado*. An 1852 sketch by Arthur Schott, as well as later excavation, showed the walled fortress to have been diamond-shaped with a circular tower and, at a corner, an angular bastion. One large building, likely the chapel, fronted the river; to the east, the imposing battlement of the Sierra del Carmen loomed up before it.

In 1777, Jose Rubio found San Vicente and other presidios already in disarray. He discovered outmoded weapons, corrupt and incompetent officers who confiscated a percentage of the garrison's always-lagging pay, undisciplined soldiers, and slow communication. In fact, he reported, it was questionable whether hostile Indians or the soldiers themselves posed the greater problem. The garrison

The Lost Chisos Mine

at San Vicente certainly did not seek out Indians to fight; on the contrary, life at the presidio was quiet and lonely for the most part. Living with their families in individual homes, officers and soldiers worked their crops and herded flocks of goats. Infrequently, they drilled, and only rarely did they skirmish Indians.

Those are the garrison's documented activities, for the most part mundane and repetitious. Legend, however, holds that the men of Presidio de San Vicente did more—much more. Two hundred years of stories charge that they looked northwest to the Chisos and found rich veins of gold or silver; some versions maintain the mine proved impractical to work, others, that a more dramatic reason existed for its loss to history.

Those mountains long had been known as the homeland of a particular Apache tribe known as the Chisos Apaches (hence, perhaps, another source of the range's name). The *viejos* ("old ones") along both sides of the Rio Grande still tell a tale when the sun drops behind the western crags: of how the soldiers of San Vicente enslaved the Chisos Apaches—or, perhaps, Indians of a friendly tribe—and marched them into the fastness of those mountains to work the mine. Subjected to cruelties and death, the Indians rebelled, massacring their captors and sealing the entrance.

Several versions of the story have been passed down through the centuries. Juan Gamboa, born in Fort Stockton in 1890, moved to Rancho Polvo, or San Vicente village a mile downstream of the presidio, in 1923 to farm and work *candelilla*. From the *viejos*— possibly direct descendants of the friendly Indians who had been infused with Spanish blood during the brief occupancy of the presidio in the 1770s—he came to know the mine as the *Escondido*, or hideout. He recounted:

> Back in the old days the Indians made horseshoes from silver. In the Chisos Mountains in Big Bend National Park there is a mine which the Spaniards worked. The mine is said to have been directly across from the presidio mission. The Spaniards used Indian labor and

blindfolded them to and from the mission. From the mission there was a tunnel to the river which the Spaniards used to keep from being attacked by Indians. That tunnel is still there hid or buried somewhere. There was a bridge made of wood across a very deep canyon, or crevice, which separated the mine from the outside. The bridge is no longer there, although there should be a path to the mine.

Gamboa's son-in-law Simon Bernal learned other details from *viejos* when he moved to San Vicente village in about 1935. A depression still evident at that time just outside the presidio's southwest corner, he noted, marked the one-time entrance to the tunnel. He recalled: "The Spaniards had Indians or prisoners, and they marched them across to a mine in the Chisos of perhaps both gold and silver. They had to cross a primitive footbridge and follow hand-chiseled steps to climb up into the high mountains and on to the mine."

But the story of the Chisos Mine did not end there, according to the account James Owens gained from old-time Big Bend ranchers Ira Hector and Homer Wilson in the mid-1930s. Owens, who served in the Chisos Basin with the Civilian Conservation Corps at that time, recalled the following:

> They worked Indians in those mines and they'd never come out—they'd work them to death. They were the Apaches, and so they rebelled. They cornered these Mexicans [or Spaniards] with twenty jackloads of gold or silver up there in one of those box canyons in the Chisos, and killed them all. And then they ran these jacks over the side of the cliff. And to get out of the canyon themselves, they had to climb the cliffs. The Indians were able to escape, and they created a tremendous rock slide in the process; they did it deliberately. And it covered over the Lost Chisos Mine.

9

The Lost Chisos Mine

The massacre well may have caused the Chisos to become associated with the notion of bewitchment or ghosts. Said Owens, "The story is, on moonlight nights, back up in the crags, you can see these [Spaniards] running from rock to rock, trying to avoid these Indians. You can see the shadows as they flit back and forth between the rocks and the boulders [that] stand up on Pulliam Peak as well as over on Casa Grande and then around up toward Toll Mountain."

Too, legend holds, in a small cave on a Chisos formation known as the Watchman's House dwells the ghost of an Indian slave charged with guarding the lost mine. Furthermore, another possible root of the word *Chisos* is the plural form of *chis*, once claimed by an old Mexican to be an Apache word meaning "clash of arms in battle," and so-applied to that range because sounds of that terrible fight between Spanish captors and rebellious Indians still echo across the mountains.

Extant Spanish reports fail to mention any such accounts of a Chisos mine and cruelties to Indian laborers, though *something* worthy of the Apache's wrath evidently happened. In 1777, Coahuila's governor reported that raids actually had intensified since the establishment of San Vicente and other presidios. The situation prompted Teodoro de Croix, commander general of the frontier provinces, to inspect the presidios of San Vicente and San Carlos in early 1778.

De Croix determined that their frontier positions along the Rio Grande left the distant settlements in present-day Mexico unguarded. He considered presidio officers' suggestions for a three thousand-soldier campaign against the Apaches, but with the outbreak of war between Spain and England in 1779 those plans were abandoned. The result was that de Croix, in that year, ordered the garrisons of San Vicente and San Carlos be moved but the physical plants retained for outpost use by roving troops.

By the time of Coahuila Governor Juan de Ugalde's campaign against Apaches in 1781, San Vicente had become a ghost—but one, perhaps, harboring a dark secret possibly not realized even by

New Spain's high command. What Ugalde did learn, however, was that Indians had torched the presidio, burning the roof and main gate. Could this act have come as retribution for the indignities heaped upon their people by greedy Spaniards gutting the Chisos of its spirit? It is a question still unanswered, but the fact remains that San Vicente—whether because of a factual "lost mine" or otherwise—never was forgotten as the decades and centuries passed.

In approximately 1783 a Spanish cartographer accurately pinpointed its location on a map of the Big Bend. In March 1787 Ugalde, undertaking his most extensive campaign against the Apaches, reached San Vicente and attacked a Mescalero band led by Zapato Tuerto in the Chisos Mountains. In 1851 Colonel Emilio Langberg, inspector of the military colonies of Chihuahua, found the chapel still standing and evidence that Comanches and Mescaleros had camped frequently inside the presidio walls. In 1852 T. W. Chandler of the U.S. and Mexican Boundary Commission navigated the Rio Grande to burst upon the edifice and note its appearance:

> On a high mesa of gravel, some sixty feet above the level of the river bottom, is situated the old presidio of San Vincente [sic], one of the ancient military posts that marked the Spanish rule in this country, long since abandoned; the adobe walls are crumbling to decay, and scarcely a stick of timber remains in the whole enclosure, except in that part devoted to the chapel.

On July 18, 1859, a grassy area immediately across the Rio Grande from San Vicente marked the camp of a twenty-four-camel United States Army contingent in the charge of Second Lieutenant William H. Echols. Forty years later, Robert T. Hill and a United States Geological Survey expedition dared the uncharted Rio Grande canyons by wooden boat to reach the presidio and record the following:

11
The Lost Chisos Mine

. . . At noon we found ourselves . . . near the ruins of the old Mexican Presidio de San Vincente [*sic*]. . . . They consist of extensive roofless walls of old adobe buildings standing in an uninhabited region, upon a low mesa a mile or two from the river. The people of the Big Bend region have a tradition that in the days of the Spanish regime they were the site of a prison

Lost Mine Peak as viewed from the Chisos highcountry to the west.

where convicts were kept and worked in certain mythical mines in the Chisos Mountains.

In 1920, said Juan Gamboa, individuals removed all doors and timbers from the presidio mission for use in Puerto Rico, site of a mine five miles southeast of Boquillas, Mexico. It plunged the ruins further into disarray, but the legend of the Lost Chisos Mine only grew stronger. By the 1930s, recounted James Owens, one particular pinnacle already had long been rumored to conceal the legendary Chisos diggings—the so-called Lost Mine Peak. Jutting second-highest in the range at 7,550 feet (only Emory rears higher), it lies approximately eighteen and one-half miles northwest of the site of Presidio de San Vicente. When viewed from the old mission, it looms directly over 4,104-foot Chilicotal Mountain to blend with a spur of 7,186-foot Crown Mountain.

The Chisos Mountains and Rio Grande as viewed from near Presidio de San Vincente.

An often-told story in the Big Bend is that if a person stands in the doorway of the old chapel at sunrise on Easter morning, he will see the first rays of the rising sun strike the Chisos either at the sealed entrance to the mine, or at the top of the peak which holds the mine at its base. Big Bend pioneer Thomas B. Henderson, upon crossing over to San Vicente village in the summer of 1924, heard a variation of the appointed date. He recalled:

> That story about where that lost mine was was talked up and down the river [Rio Grande]. We asked an old Mexican at San Vicente if he knew anything about that. He told us they decided it was a Wednesday in May; they said when the sun came up, the first place it hit was right at the entrance to that cave. He said they put men up there before Wednesday to try and locate where the sun first hit [the Chisos]. Well, when the sun first hit it, it hit the whole side of the mountain.

The latter account is similar to another directional clue which maintains that a person must stand in the opening of the old Boquillas (Puerto Rico) mine on the thirteenth, or seventeenth, of May in order to see the initial rays illuminate the proper mountain.

Considering the fact that Lost Mine Peak is 285 feet lower than 7,835-foot Emory Peak three and one-half miles to the southwest, some persons dispute the claim that a rising sun *ever* could first strike any part of the Chisos other than Emory, the range's highest point. That argument, however, is based on the assumption that the sun rises from a smooth horizon. The fact is, throughout May or on any given Easter—and that day could range from March 22 through April 25—the sun comes up over the great wall of Mexico's Sierra del Carmen, whose serrated crest possibly could dictate directional rays for a short time. With Lost Mine Peak lying on a latitude slightly more than two miles north of Emory, it *is* conceivable that, on one particular day between March 22 and May 31, the first rays of the sun momentarily could strike Lost Mine Peak before Emory.

The palisaded pinnacle of Emory Peak.

Some evidence, however, supports the theory that the Chisos Mine indeed lies hidden on Emory. When Simon Bernal was living in San Vicente village and herding goats in the vicinity of the mission ruins, he sometimes looked toward the Chisos and remembered what the *viejos* had told him: To find the lost mine, stand at the adobe ruins and study the Chisos in the distance; where the mountains appear whitest, the mine lies concealed. Depending on the time of day and year, that area could be Lost Mine Peak, Crown Mountain, Pummel Peak—or Emory, which assuredly bears a diadem of sheer, white rock, although more starkly on the west than on the San Vicente side.

On Emory's east face, where the mountain makes a great thrust skyward to hold dominion over the talus slopes, forested rim, and lesser peaks below, James Owens stumbled upon an intriguing topographical feature in the mid-1930s. It was a cave, or opening, extending back into the mountain and then plunging, as later speleological study revealed, to an ultimate vertical depth of two hundred feet. Owens recalled:

> It's two-thirds of the way up, at the bottom of an upthrust. There are two large piñon trees, old ones, standing there right by it. It's hard to find, but we used to go up in there. You had to bend over a little. There were some timbers in it, and we used those logs to scramble down from one level to the next, going down about three levels. I took the commanding officer of that CCC company and his executive officer and let them go in. I'd been in it enough, so I just stayed on the outside. They went in that cave and directly [occurred] the biggest commotion you ever heard. Boy, they came out of there. One went down this way and this other guy went down that way, and out came a two-thirds- or half-grown bear trying to get out of the place.

Owens initially believed the opening to be an "orifice or a volcanic vent," but he conceded that "there might've been people digging in there at one time." The fact timbers already were present lends an ever-so-slight hint they might once have been support beams—a suggestion Owens could neither substantiate nor refute by the inadequate light of a small flashlight.

From old-time Big Bend ranchers in the 1930s Owens heard a different version of the directional clue, one which, if true, would place the mine at neither Lost Mine Peak nor Emory, but southward in the lesser and more barren Chisos peaks known as Sierra Quemada. Said Owens, "You can stand in the old mission at San Vicente in the afternoon [of a certain day] in August, and whenever the sun goes down, it's supposed to go down between two peaks. And at the base of those peaks is where this mine exists."

The August sun, he added, would set generally behind 5,240-foot Elephant Tusk.

Adrenalin-pumping legends of concealed mines and the clues by which they may be found often crumble before the scrutiny of historians demanding documented facts. Is it so in the case of the Lost Chisos Mine?

That Spaniards sought silver and gold in North America is unquestioned. That they occasionally enslaved Indians to work mines also is established, as is the fact that captive Indians were inclined to revolt and destroy all evidences of mines so they never could be forced to work them again. Too, unlike some regions with alleged lost mines, the Big Bend *does* hold precious metals. The old Shafter mine eighty miles northwest of the Chisos yielded silver as early as the 1860s. The Puerto Rico Mine, established by 1894 five miles southeast of Boquillas at the base of the Sierra del Carmen, held deposits of lead, silver, and zinc. That same year saw quicksilver mining initiated near Terlingua, sixteen miles west-northwest of the Chisos. The Mariscal quicksilver mine, dating to the late 1890s, lay only a dozen miles southeast of Emory Peak.

Moreover, the Lost Chisos Mine is not alone among lost treasures or concealed diggings in the Chisos area. Simon Bernal, once of San Vicente, related the account of a horseman riding to one of five springs at the base of the Chisos; at that unknown spring, he discovered gold nuggets lodged in his horse's shoe.

From the *viejos* of the dozen families which composed San Vicente village, Bernal also heard the story of the Lost Thirty-Four Mine, or *"La Bibiana"* (in Spanish, a female proper name), said to lie just north of 3,940-foot Mariscal Mountain. His uncle, Gumesindo Sanchez of San Vicente, was riding horseback through that area one day when the ground suddenly collapsed beneath his horse's leg. After the animal extricated itself, Sanchez looked back to see a deep cavity with support beams. Not realizing he may have stumbled upon *La Bibiana*, he rode onward. Later, understanding the possible significance of his find, he returned to discover that someone had widened the opening and evidently removed its contents.

The Chisos range itself is an unlikely site for gold or silver, say geologists, as its higher rocks are volcanic lavas which do not commonly yield precious metals. However, a few small intrusions suggesting the possibility of silver or gold do exist in the Chisos. Too, rancher W. T. Burnham claimed to have found a crudely molded bar of silver near Lost Mine Peak sometime after 1914. Fellow rancher Homer Wilson told James Owens he had discovered a gold nugget the size of a blackeyed pea in Oak Creek in the Chisos Basin. And in the 1910s the east side of Ward Mountain was mined for gold, with assays by American Metals Company allegedly indicating traces of the metal.

Furthermore, the Spaniards supposedly had a well-established trail from the presidio to the mine, according to the account Juan Gamboa first heard in San Vicente village in the 1920s. Indeed, an old trail known as Smuggler's, or Contraband Trail *does* lead from the vicinity of the old presidio, through desert crags, and

Lost Mine Peak as seen from across Juniper Canyon.

up Juniper Canyon in the Chisos before all signs of it vanish. And along the upper reaches of that trail, rancher Lloyd Wade found a silver bar prior to 1934 and related the find to James Owens.

But, for every Big Bend native who has found hints of the Lost Chisos Mine, there are others who doubt its existence. Francis Rooney, for example, lived just below the pour-off of the Chisos Basin Window for several years beginning in 1912, yet held only skepticism regarding a supposed mine. In 1990 he recalled: "I've heard about it all my life. I was just a kid [in 1912] and now I'm ninety-one years old, and I know no more about it today than I did then."

Thus, the jury stands silent on the legend of the Lost Chisos Mine, as it has for two centuries. If it ever did exist, no trace of it remains to tempt modern-day Coronados. Yet, there are those who still wonder, who still seek.

The ruins of Presidio de San Vicente, meanwhile, rise stoically to face the mysterious Chisos range against the horizon. Villagers shun its crumbling walls after sunset; the *viejos* explain that it is because the ancient fortress is haunted by La Llorona, the woman in white who drowned her children and is doomed to walk the night, crying and searching for them.

Several years ago, two vacationing Americans aware of the old mission's directional clues dared spend the night under its walls. They were awakened at midnight in the pitch black of that deserted ruin by the eerie sound of bells tolling. It drove them fleeing like the shadows of ghostly Spaniards flitting among the boulders of the Chisos.

Perhaps the guarding spirits of San Vicente deem the secret of the Lost Chisos Mine one better left alone.

Phantoms and Ghost Lights

𖠿

𝓡estless and crying, they may still wander the dark night in a foredoomed quest for peace.

They are the indigenous spirits and devils known to early Texas pioneers, and for many persons today, they are more than myths; they are real, transcending ethnic lines.

For descendants of the Mexican Indians who settled along the West Texas-Mexico border, the best-known wandering spirit is La Llorona, the crying woman dressed in white. Folklorists hold that the legend originated as an Aztec story regarding a white-adorned goddess who carried on her shoulders a cradle apparently bearing a child. When she abandoned the cradle among Aztec women, they found it empty but for an arrow point shaped like a sacrificial knife. Thereafter, the Aztecs would hear her crying as she paced the nights prior to vanishing into a river or lake.

Folklorists further contend that in the sixteenth century the base legend merged with a second story of Mexico: Luisa, beautiful but a peasant, bore three sons to Don Muño Montes Claros of the upper class. When he forsook her to marry a woman of his own stature, Luisa slew the children and ran through the streets wailing and screaming. Learning of the tragedy, Don Muño committed suicide.

With retelling over the centuries, the accounts evolved along the Texas-Mexico border into the story of La Llorona. Though many variations exist, each adapted to the topography of a specific locale, the most common version today holds that La Llorona, once a loving mother, went crazy and drowned her seven children.

Doomed never to rest until she finds and restores them, she wanders the night crying for her babies. Because water precipitated her evil deed, she often frequents waterways or other water sources. Fort Stockton residents Rose Duarte and Gloria Dupre recounted the tale that La Llorona often is seen wandering the Fort Stockton park which comprises historic Comanche Springs, long an important landmark on the Comanche War Trail.

Deeper in the Chihuahuan Desert, where water is a rare commodity, La Llorona had no choice but to seek other methods of infanticide. James Owens heard a variation while stationed with the Civilian Conservation Corps in the Basin of now-Big Bend National Park from 1934 to 1936: "This story was that there were some Mexicans living up in the Chisos [Mountains], and one of the women was pregnant," recounted Owens.

And during her pregnancy she saw a six-striped lizard, which was an ill-omen that evil would possess the children when they were born. When her children were born, she took her babes in arms and went up on Pulliam Bluff and threw them over the bluff.

Now, the wind blows through there; you can hear some moaning sounds if you're listening. And so the story goes that now as you come up through there at certain times, you can hear this moaning of the mother, and the occasional crying of a child when she threw them over the bluff.

Not surprisingly, La Llorona is associated with cemeteries as well as waterways and cliffs. One such site is St. Joseph's Catholic Cemetery in Fort Stockton. "The kids go down to the cemetery and wait, and they will swear that they have seen a beautiful woman, and she wears a long white gown and has long flowing hair," said researcher Lee Harris of Fort Stockton. "She strolls around there. You'll just catch a few glimpses of her, they say. And these are not just the Mexican American people; these are the Anglo kids too."

St. Joseph's Catholic Cemetery in Fort Stockton.

Though a product of Mexican American culture, La Llorona is not bound by ethnicity; the modern era's "vanishing hitchhiker" variant, for example, has been reported by persons of widely diverse national origin. Too, she has not been limited to West Texas.

Deep in the piney woods of East Texas's Henderson County in approximately 1915, Lucy B. Dearen, her husband, and their infants had an encounter which could be interpreted as a brush with La Llorona. The time was late at night, the setting, a remote and shadowy lane shrouded on either side by overhanging timber. And down it creaked the Dearens' buggy, pulled by a big bay horse.

Old Bill, as they called him, was far from fearless. In fact, he was so skittish that even a feather fluttering in a weed would spook him. On a prior occasion, Mrs. Dearen had pulled Old Bill to a halt before a neighbor's house and sat waiting in the buggy when the horse grew frightened at this least of menaces.

"There was bermuda grass all out in front of the house, and the lady had chickens," recalled Mrs. Dearen. "Well, a feather . . .

Lucy B. Dearen

caught in a weed out there and he noticed it. And he pricked his ears, and he began to bounce and to bounce. And I couldn't do a thing on earth with him. And [my relative] came and she got in the buggy, and we got out of there—and Old Bill didn't stop till he got to the [home] gate."

It was this equine sensitivity to anything out of the ordinary that made the forthcoming incident in the shadowy country lane so eerie.

"We went to Mama's, and we always came home after night, in a buggy," she remembered.

It was in the Kickapoo Bottom . . . and a tree about [two feet] around had fell down across the road. And somebody'd just taken the saw and sawed the hunk out in the middle of the road. Well, we were coming on, going home, and I saw the woman—she had great long hair and she was dressed in white. And Pa [saw her] too. And I said, "Look a-yonder at that woman. I'll bet you Old Bill don't go by *that*."

Well, he just went right on by; he didn't pay a bit of attention to anything. Old Bill would get scared of a *feather*, and he didn't pay a bit of mind to her. And there she sat where the log was; she was just sitting there in that white dress and her long black hair. I could've reached out and touched her with my hand. She didn't say a word and we didn't either. And Pa whipped Old Bill up just a little bit.

This mysterious woman-beside-the-road still was making herself known in the 1960s, this time to an Imperial man driving Highway 1053 between Fort Stockton and Imperial. According to Lee Harris, who gained her information from a close friend of the man, La Llorona lay in wait repeatedly for the driver in the borrow ditch at a point just past Burleson's Trucking Company north of Fort Stockton; the encounters always were at night.

"She would be standing by the side of the road," narrated Mrs. Harris.

And she would just attach herself to the car and ride, and then just get off. That was the only car she ever bothered, but it did not matter whether there was some-one in the car with him or not. And this [eyewitness information] has come from Imperial residents too. She would never get on the car when he came to Fort Stockton; she seemed to know when he was here and would be waiting for him. He would drive a hundred miles an hour going back to Imperial, but he absolutely hated to come to Fort Stockton because invariably she would attach herself to his car and ride for about ten miles. The man was finally killed in a plane crash . . . in the late sixties.

That particular stretch of country along Highway 1053 long has been known as an area frequented by La Llorona. Near a hill rising a few miles north of Fort Stockton and adjacent to the highway, Rose Duarte's great-uncle met La Llorona in a terrifying way back in pioneer days.

"Where that hill is, there's a ranch, and if you cross it at night you'll see La Llorona," said Miss Duarte.

Dad said his uncle was going to this ranch, but they were scared to go through there in the buggy; they'd be going, and the lady [La Llorona] would appear right next to it. He said one day his uncle was coming from town, and he turned around and this lady was sitting right beside him. He just fell over, and that horse, so used to going from here to there, just took him all the way home. He told my aunt, "I saw this lady right next to me all dressed in white." And apparently he saw a face and everything.

That same hill also has been associated with reports of mysterious lights. In Mexican American culture, such a phenomenon often is linked to buried treasure, with the intensity of the light in direct correlation to the size of the bonanza. One Pecos County man who witnessed inexplicable lights on his property near Fort Stockton believed unquestionably that treasure lurked near.

When Eduardo Duarte was ten years old back in 1925, said his daughter Rose Duarte, he and his family farmed near Fort Stockton. One night, young Eduardo was accompanying his father toward a bridge behind the farm when the boy heard the rhythmic strike of shovel against rock—in Mexican American folklore, the unmistakable sound of a treasure making itself known.

"My grandpa said, 'No, you didn't hear nothing; there's nothing,'" narrated Miss Duarte.

Well, they went back [home], and when Dad fell asleep, my grandfather got up. He didn't show up the next morning; they couldn't find him. So Dad went out to feed the cattle and horses and he couldn't find the shovel. So he remembered that thing [from the night before], and circled around till he came up there—and there was a spot, so big, dug out. It was shaped just like a box. The shovel was there, the crowbar, and some other tool.

So that night, as soon as the sun was going down, his dad drove up and said, "You don't have to work no more. Everybody get in that car; we'll just go live with someone." He found treasure. Nobody knows what he did with it. And they came to live with Chino Duarte, but my grandfather went crazy. He just kept saying that he didn't have to work no more, that he's done it despite everything in the world. They say that when you open treasure like that—it's supposed to be gold—it's got gases. And when he opened that thing, he got it right in his eye, on his face. I don't know if it's got anything to do with it, but they said that's why he went crazy.

And so her grandfather died without ever revealing the site of the treasure, which he apparently had relocated somewhere on that five-and-a-half-acre family farm just outside Fort Stockton.

"That money is buried some place out there on Dad's property," said Miss Duarte. In fact, she added, it has revealed itself to him on occasion by lights and noises.

"He's seen that light twice, and it's a perfectly square light," she noted.

Once they were right there in the house, and my father and my brother both saw it, and they started running to it. They got about halfway and it was gone. Also, on out there at the house we leave the windows open in summertime, and if it's real quiet, you can hear a sound like when you open a can, kind of a *pssst!* In summertime, you can hear it just as plain as ever. And it's coming from the same direction as that light. But it's strange, 'cause every time he tries to dig [the treasure] up, something always comes up; he always gets sick or something.

Mystery lights abound in the Pecos country, but none is more intriguing than the ghost fires which dance at night out across arid flats and craggy mountains of the Big Bend.

They flare suddenly out of a black veil, to loom as fiery eyes staring from afar. They may pulsate or divide, or crawl against a dark horizon where no man-made light ever has been. And they still mystify and mesmerize just as greatly as when Big Bend pioneers first stared into the night and found fires which burned but did not consume.

Two mountain ranges in particular long have been associated with the "ghost lights"—the Dead Horse Mountains (Sierra del Caballo Muerto) and the Chinati Mountains. A third range, the Chisos, also has been linked to mysterious lights.

The Dead Horse Mountains, as eerie as their name is macabre, rise in Mexico as the mighty Sierra del Carmen and thrust northward to crest barren and bone-dry at 5,854-foot Sue Peaks in Brewster County. Thomas B. Henderson, born in 1908, grew up on Maravillas Creek in the shadow of that range. From the Henderson ranch approximately six miles east of Persimmon Gap, he and his family first sighted the Dead Horse lights in 1914—an unusually wet year for the Chihuahuan Desert. The flares, he said, would appear in the general area of Big Brushy Canyon, which heads in the Dead Horse range and runs north-northwest sixteen miles to intersect Maravillas Creek three miles east of the old Henderson place.

"Up there in Brushy Canyon, on the east side of the Dead Horses, there's kind of a bluff-looking thing, like a rock slide," Henderson recalled. "Every time it would come a lightning storm over in that area, that light would come on. If [it would] sprinkle a little bit, and thunder and lightning, you could see the flashes. We were twenty-five miles or so from that place. When it quit raining, quit lightning, that light would stay there. When we went to bed pretty late, it would still be burning. There on our front porch we watched it many a night, and we always speculated on what made it. But in the morning it wouldn't be there."

Henderson described the light as fire-like in appearance, yet unlike a true fire because it continued to flare through driving rainstorms. "You've seen trash fires that blaze up here a little bit, and then blaze up over there—it was something like that," he said.

Curiosity finally prompted the Hendersons to try to pinpoint the light's source.

"We nailed a board on the porch post and fixed a rifle on it," he recalled. "It had a peep sight, which wasn't much bigger than a broom straw. And we sighted down through those sights at that fire. Our house was facing due east, right on the compass. And [the fire] was a little bit to the right of east. It wasn't much—I'd say fifteen or twenty degrees. You could see it kind of blaze up here and over there and kind of dance back and forth like it was really burning."

Keeping the firearm affixed to the post all night, they returned to look down the sights by day. "You know what we saw the next morning? We saw the Dead Horse Mountains. We couldn't pinpoint anything."

The Dead Horse light revealed itself to Henderson sporadically over the decades, appearing only every four or five years during wet seasons that fostered sightings by other ranching families as well. W. R. Green witnessed unusual lights in the range as early as 1912, when at age six he moved with his family to Maravillas Creek. From there, and from his later homes in the 1910s at Dugout Wells and McKinney Springs, he could see the mountains ablaze with fires in damp weather.

Thomas B. Henderson

"It was just like a light, a coal oil lamp or something, and you could see it jump up," Green recalled. "You'd see lights different places; there's more than one. It had to be snowing or some kind of damp weather before they'd show up."

Green viewed similar nocturnal lights in several craggy ranges, including the Chisos, which jut to 7,835 feet in present-day

Big Bend National Park: "[They] looked like they were two or three hundred feet high, around the Chisos Mountains," he said. "But there's more in the Dead Horse Mountains. If the wind was blowing, they'd turn over, whichever way the wind was blowing. But if it was still, they'd just go up. There were big ones, and some of them [were] just little ones."

W. R. Green

Unlike many legends spawned in pioneer days, the ghost lights of Brewster County have not vanished into folklore. "People still see it when it tries to rain over there," said Henderson in 1990.

Away to the west between the Davis and Chinati mountains, the so-called "Marfa Lights" continue to tease and elude after more than a century. Early Trans-Pecos settler Robert Ellison claimed to have seen the lights on his second night in the Big Bend in 1883. Driving cattle west through 5,067-foot Paisano Pass from the railroad station at present-day Alpine, Ellison burst upon a high, open plateau—Mitchell Flat—and mistook the lights for the campfires of Apaches.

To the casual observer, positioned after sundown at Paisano Pass or at the entrance to abandoned Marfa Army Air Base four miles westward down U.S. 67-90, the lights generally appear as distant flares that move and divide against the 7,730-foot Chinatis and their foothills on the south-southwestern horizon. Occasionally, stationary lights are visible directly to the south, and, rarely, these southern lights will be seen bounding through the arid flats.

Rarest of all, though, are "close encounters," when the lights supposedly seek out individuals daring the Trans-Pecos dark. One such incident involved Lou Ashmore and her daughter Alice in the summer of 1966. A Sul Ross State College student seeking to complement her degree in geology, Mrs. Ashmore frequently ventured onto the abandoned runways of the air base to view the mysterious lights. One particular night found the Ashmores and a girlfriend and her young son parked just off a runway on a dirt road leading south. It was eleven p.m., and ever since nightfall they had sat in their car and watched the lights flare and dance against the black horizon.

"You'll see them up on the mountains: three here, one at a lower elevation here, and then one way down at the base of the range," said Mrs. Ashmore. "They're never the same. They

The Chinati Mountains as viewed from the west.

appear to move, sometimes vertically, but more horizontally. They divide and turn colors. Sometimes one will come on very bright, and then there'll be two not very bright, or there'll be three very bright."

It was just that kind of varied, faraway display they had watched all evening—until suddenly the darkness split and something seemed to be racing toward them out of the south.

"They do come down off the mountains and come in at lower elevations, and this one was a very bright light, a white light," Mrs. Ashmore remembered. "And it did seem to be larger, and it was moving toward us at an angle. It was moving in, what I thought was very close to us."

Her daughter Alice, who was eight at the time, recalled the phenomenon as an adult:

I remember the light being very close and very bright; it was pretty awe-inspiring. It seemed like it was maybe not more than a half-mile away. And I remember my mother [and her friend] both got very, very excited when it came on us: *"Aaaa! Look at that!"* This one was much larger and much brighter. It didn't have any color, and a lot of times they'll be green or even have a reddish cast. It was a very white, bright light that was more intense in the center and more diffuse around the edges. As it came in, it stayed the same size; no matter how close or how far away it got, it stayed the same size. It looked a good three to four feet in diameter, and it just moved in and grew very bright and was sort of stationary; it was like a staring contest between us.

Unlike her mother, who found the light "playful and curious" rather than threatening, Alice became terrified. "It really frightened [the boy] and I, it was so close. There was a blanket in the back seat, and we hid under the blanket because we just knew that whatever it was, it was going to come through the car and singe us. And I've never had that feeling before or since."

In the minute or two that Lou Ashmore stared spellbound at the light hovering just above that dark road, she gained the distinct sensation of a lurking intelligence. "I had a feeling," she recalled, "the light was smarter than I was and was not going to be found out by me or anyone else."

But that did not deter her from trying. Starting the engine, she gunned the Buick Wildcat straight toward that mysterious light. The vehicle reached speeds of fifty miles per hour on that primitive road, and even above the glare of her headlights the great light loomed brilliant against the black of night.

"I was so intent on this light that I really don't know whether it stopped, or appeared to come in and move away, before I started following it," she detailed. "I thought, 'This time it's there, and I'm going to see it.' I tracked it to the south. As I went toward it, it moved away from me, right directly in front of me, just as fast as I was going, to always stay the same distance ahead of me. It moved at great speed."

"It moved away just as fast as she could chase it," corroborated Alice. "And [the boy] and I were in the back seat howling like banshees, scared to death."

Finding herself no closer to the light after a frenzied chase of one and a half to two miles, Lou Ashmore yielded to the pleas of the children and applied the brakes—just in time to avoid crashing into a locked gate. There the four of them sat, aware that they had just brushed shoulders with a legend.

"When I stopped, the light kept on going, right to the south quite a ways," she recounted. "It stayed around and then it just turned off."

Though the Ashmores experienced the Big Bend ghost fires in a way few persons ever have, they could offer no better explanation for their source other than possible manifestations of angels. Scientists and academics, however, have not been at a loss to tender theories, including swamp gas (in a region arid in the extreme), static electricity discharges akin to St. Elmo's fire, jackrabbits bearing phosphorescent particles, moonlight playing on undiscovered mica beds, and the phosphate of bat guano reacting with moisture.

Dr. John Desmond, onetime geology professor at Sul Ross, believed phosphorescent minerals, subjected to certain radiation, spawn the displays. "Cosmic rays from outer space may cause the radiation," he noted.

James Owens, intimate with the Big Bend from 1934 on, considered the possibility the lights are the result of certain algae phosphorescing. "The algae that grows on those rocks will phosphoresce at a certain stage of growth and under a certain given set of conditions, with moisture," explained Owens, who taught microbiology and chemistry at Howard College at Big Spring. "I have found small plants back up in the Chisos there that would more or less phosphoresce. As far as lighting up that whole area, that could happen; it's a possibility."

The most common scientific explanation, however, involves vehicle headlights or heavenly bodies. Public relations officials with McDonald Observatory, situated on Mount Locke on the upper fringe of the Big Bend, have gone on record as stating the lights are the result of the Novaya Zemlya effect. An article in the June 1987 issue of the official observatory publication *Star Date* explained this atmospheric phenomenon as a bending of light rays (originating at a distant point) when they strike a boundary between cold air hugging the ground and warm air hovering above.

"Headlights of cars on roads south of the plains southwest of Marfa are normally not visible," stated the article, penned by Diana Hadley. "However, when a layer of cold air forms over the southwest plains, the headlight beams are bent back toward the earth and thus visible to observers on Highway 67 [90] and Mitchell Mesa east of Marfa."

The author went on to state that the lights appear to be coming from the sky and move around and change "both because the properties of the boundary layer are changing and because the cars are moving. Of course, any stars and planets near the horizon, to the south of Marfa, will be affected in the same way."

Though backed by a respected scientific institution, this theory nevertheless is subject to debate. The lights are reported on overcast nights as well as on starry ones, casting serious doubts that stars and planets are responsible. The headlight hypothesis, meanwhile, would seem to hold much substance—until one considers not only how rare autos were in the Big Bend when Green and Henderson first sighted the fires in the early 1910s, but how utterly impossible the prospect was when Ellison viewed them in the 1880s. Ellison, in fact, became incensed when a later generation suggested that car lights were the source of the phenomena. "Automobiles in this country in 1883 were pretty damned scarce," he snapped.

While the Big Bend ghost fires continue to loom as elusive and wispy as when Robert Ellison first sighted them, other ghostly guardians of the Pecos country assume more material forms. Six miles northwest of present-day Andrews, for example, a white-shrouded playa two miles wide is said to witness the annual ride of a headless horseman. Some say he is Colonel William Shafter—the lake now bears his name—and that in its mire his contingent lost wagonloads of gold. Shafter, along with nine troops of cavalry and sixty-four wagons, came this way on a major scouting expedition in 1875.

"Colonel Shafter and them were bringing gold across, and the Indians started chasing them," recounted Lee Ann Ballew, who heard the tale from her mother, Virginia Irwin. "[Shafter and his party] ran out onto the lake thinking they could cross, because it's got all this salt and looks like it would hold you up. They got out so far and [the gold] sank down in the quicksand."

In his official report, Shafter did not mention gold, and noted no military casualties and only one Indian killed and five captured in the entire five-month campaign. Lost treasures, however, do not respect documented history any better than spooks do. And so it is, related Virginia Irwin, that at high noon every December twelfth—"the twelfth hour of the twelfth day of the twelfth month"—the headless horseman returns to Shafter Lake in quest of the head he presumably lost in that legendary battle.

Less clear, however, is the purpose of a supernatural winged creature in a Fort Stockton neighborhood known as Little Mexico, where dark nights find it sentineling a set of unstable adobe walls.

"It's right by the old Spanish church that is in Little Mexico," said Lee Harris. "There's a bunch of vacant pastures there and some crumbling walls. Tradition through the youth is that there is a great big phoenix [or *lechuza*] that rises from it. The children will go out and lay at night watching for the bird to come out of this. Rarely ever will a child stay out there by himself to see the phoenix rise. They say the wing span is at least thirty-six feet."

While a *lechuza* is supposedly a manifestation of a *bruja* (witch), not all spirits reported in West Texas are malevolent. On a "beautiful moonlit night"—April 8, 1958—Ortha Huff of San Angelo took a hot shower and went to bed about eleven o'clock. She was lying

The adobe walls from which the ghost bird is said to rise.

with her right arm over her head and her left arm across her chest. Finding a comfortable sleeping position was difficult; neither doctors nor chiropractors had been able to treat her painful back injury dating to the early 1940s or the intense arthritis in her spine. Suddenly, she recalled, from out of the dark an arm from elbow to fingertips appeared in front of her. It was brightly illuminated and adorned in a white, wavy slip with open cuff dangling, and when three fingers of the hand touched Mrs. Huff on the elbow she jumped and the arm disappeared.

A sensation of great warmth surged through her entire body, she said, and then "the Lord appeared" at the left of her bed. She described the figure as full-sized, dressed in a "beautiful white robe" and illuminated in a light "so bright it was blue." He had a clear face with ruddy complexion, a straight sharp nose, small mustache, and long auburn hair parted on the left. His hands were clasped in front of Him "like a person would if he was talking to someone."

The figure remained at her bedside for "one or two minutes," although no words were spoken. "I was too petrified," said Mrs. Huff.

When the figure disappeared, all the pain in her back left "and from that night to this day, the places that hurt me then have never hurt me since."

But where there are spirits of love, there are those so eerie that pioneers even identified them as devils or demons. Deep in the thickets of Henderson County in East Texas in the late 1880s or early 1890s, one man in particular had a life-changing encounter with something from beyond, remembered Lucy B. Dearen.

Born January 25, 1867 and christened Jessie D. Gracy, he suffered infantile paralysis as an infant and had one poorly developed leg for which he used a crutch. "Jessie was his name, Aunt Bell's brother," recalled Mrs. Dearen, who heard the story as a child in Henderson County in the 1890s.

> The [church] meeting was going on there at Martin's Mill, and Aunt Bell was a hot-headed Methodist; she believed in going to church and she thought everybody else ought to go. So they were getting ready to go, and Jessie was their baby brother and he wasn't getting ready. And she said, "Jess, aren't you going?" He said, "No, I'm going to that dance over at Flat Creek tonight." He was a grown man; I expect he was twenty-three or twenty-four years old.

Well, she cried and she begged and she pled. Nope, he wasn't a-going; he was going to that dance. So the rest of them got in the wagon . . . and they went on to church, [and] he went on to the dance; he went horseback. Church was over and they came home, went to bed.

So they'd all gone to bed—it was in the summertime—[and] about one or two o'clock, why, Jessie came in. Oh, he was in a terrible hurry. He woke one of his older brothers [and] said, "Bill! Bill, get up! I was coming home from [the dance] tonight and I met something in the middle of the road!"

He didn't simply *meet* something along that gloomy stretch of overhanging timbers, he gasped; it came spinning and tumbling right down the road toward him.

It was shaped on each end kind of like a top, and it was big like a barrel, but it was pointed! And it was going on one of those ends, then it'd drop over and go some more! It had holes bored all in it [and] had a light in it, kind of lightning, and was full of little stars all around it!"

His horse didn't notice it, didn't even move. He said he had to get off of the road to let it pass.

He watched it turn and go tumbling out into the murky thickets, then he whipped his horse all the way home.

It just liked to scared him to death, so they got some lanterns . . . and they went back up there. He showed the place where it was and there wasn't no sign of anything, only the horse's tracks.

Aunt Bell told him it was the devil after him. Well, he didn't go to any more dances when there was any meeting going on. . . . That kind of made a believer out of him. So the next night he went to church, but he went on his horse—he didn't go in the wagon with [his family]—and it got after him *again*. And [that] night he got religion.

Whatever it was that Jessie Gracy met along that dark and spooky road, it was real enough to him to affect his life profoundly—so much so, that upon his death April 22, 1900, his survivors etched in his tombstone the epitaph *He die[d] in Jesus and are blest.*

Skeptics sometimes attribute such accounts of ghostly fireballs to an often-misinterpreted phenomenon known as ball lightning. Indeed, Mrs. Dearen herself evidently witnessed an extremely rare instance of ball lightning in approximately 1912 near Martin's Mill in Van Zandt County.

"We were living in this old log house; the big room was great big . . . and we had a fireplace made out of mud and straw," she narrated. "It was in the fall of the year but we hadn't had any fire in there. . . . Anyway, we'd gone to bed that night and I woke up, and I saw the ball of fire—it just came rolling out [of the fireplace] and rolled up to the wall and rolled back."

That sphere of fire, she said, was about the size of "a half-grown watermelon [and had] spots of brightness . . . just like diamonds. It didn't burn anything."

The incident involving Jessie Gracy, however, suggests something other than ball lightning, for such a phenomenon along that otherwise pitch-black road likely would have spooked the man's horse to the point of bucking.

Conversely, though, the supposed possession of a devil, or demon, by a Pecos County bronc rider back in the nineteenth century reportedly empowered him with the ability to ride even the wildest horse effortlessly. "That man supposedly had a devil in a small jar," said Rose Duarte, who heard the story from her father. "And he was a darned good bronco rider back in the 1800s. And every time he rode one, he had the devil on top of the table, right in the middle. And he went out, and that horse would never throw that guy—never. The man just stayed on those horses and was never thrown, except for one time. The wife was cleaning the table, knocked the devil off, broke the glass, and the devil got away. And he fell and could never ride again."

Loosed a century ago, that devil still may be wandering the West Texas night, an "unclean spirit [that] passes through waterless places seeking rest, but he finds none" (Matthew 12:43). Forever searching men's souls and biding his time, he is fated either to possess, or be possessed.

Walk carefully, therefore, the gloom beyond sunset—for in the shadows may lurk dark and evil secrets.

The mysterious house cradled by peaks of the Davis Mountains.

The Davis Mountains Spirit

*H*is spectral image burned itself into her memory forever.

In the master bedroom of a Davis Mountains bungalow she lay adrift in the shadowy, in-between world that was neither sleep nor consciousness. And suddenly he stood above her, his Indian features unmistakable: squat but sinewy body, long ebony hair, high forehead, oval face, pointed chin. And from his belt hung something narrow and dark she could not quite identify—perhaps a shaman's leather pouch, maybe even scalps or a shrunken head.

The strange apparition did not have the countenance of one who threatened, but neither did it smile. It but stood stoically looking upon her just long enough for the details to flood her mind—and then it was gone.

She started, becoming fully alert. Yet, even in stark consciousness she would experience the Indian's presence many more times during the next few months.

Did a logical explanation exist, perhaps imagination and hallucination blending fantasy with reality? Or had it truly been an encounter with something from beyond, a visitation, perhaps, by a disembodied spirit or a shaman who had bridged the chasm of time?

Karen Keefe was not sure then, but later she became convinced that she had been touched by something beyond the temporal world.

From the very day Karen and her husband Forrest moved into the three-bedroom house, nestled amid rocky crags and touching the sky at six thousand feet, the bizarre and cryptic seemed to rule.

Karen and Forrest Keefe on the porch of the house.

Once, the structure had catered to aficionados of Italian and Mexican cuisine in downtown Fort Davis, but business failure had left it to be reborn in enigma seventeen miles west. There, the newlyweds—she twenty-eight, he thirty—expected to embark on a lifetime of marital bliss. But that was before they came to believe the beige house already had an occupant—and they were but intruders.

The first howls in the night presaged the mysteries to follow. They had crossed the threshold earlier that February day, and now sought to relax from the emotional pressures of working with troubled kids at High Frontier Ranch midway between Fort Davis and Alpine. Then a coyote pack descended on their home, the yelps and cries a forlorn, primeval serenade from just beyond the door. "Sounds like a bunch of wild Indians," Forrest told his wife.

Drifting away toward the gnarled ridgebacks, his words became silence, awaiting the day they would echo back into his ears.

When they would, he would not quite know how to deal with it, not one such as he who always had felt a unity with nature and its laws.

Forrest's entire life, in fact, seemed a fulfilled prophecy of his name. He grew up in the shadow of Colorado's Pike's Peak, a castellated pinnacle of forests and ice-capped tundra rising to the clouds. It was the land of Manitou Springs, where waters gushed from the earth seemingly to merge with the spiritual. In such a setting, there in Colorado Springs, a Ute Indian took him under his wing, leading the seven-year-old boy in the ways of the forest, its denizens, the firmament above.

The clouds, the sky, the birds—only *they* truly were free, unencumbered by the limitations of land-bound man. And it was through a bird of prey that the small boy was to come into close communion with the earth and its canopy and experience the freedom of spirit which the Indians believed the falcon represented.

And he learned much, this seven-year-old becoming fourteen. He discovered that, to the Indians, nature and the spirit world were closely entwined, almost inseparable. He learned that to wear the feathers of the hawk into battle was to gain strength, that to put the feathers of the falcon on an arrow empowered it with great speed and accuracy. But it was the feather of the eagle—which endowed a warrior with soaring bravery—that troubled and disheartened him when he found work as an adult at Ouray National Wildlife Refuge near Vernal, Utah.

There, he saw Ute Indians not as proud, fearless warriors, but as contradictions to their heritage. "They were all drunkards, and they just hung out at stores and they drank and they never worked," charged Forrest. "It was horrible for such a fine type of people—at one time—to live like that. I was disgusted by them. I wouldn't even talk to them."

Still, he never lost his admiration for primeval Indians; he only submerged it. The veneration quickly would resurface when he believed their spirits to summon him at the bungalow in the Davis Mountains.

He came to that range's palisaded canyons and ridges of volcanic rock as one seeking to mesh his occupation with his lifeblood. At High Frontier, six miles south of Fort Davis on Texas 118, he found it. There, at the behest of the courts and welfare agencies, youths lived to tread the unexplored frontiers of their own potentials. They were the wayward and the abandoned, the troubled and the troublemakers, and about them sprawled the Big Bend and a vastness as great as their own needs for character development—a correlation that did not escape Forrest.

Looking into his own life, he saw the inner peace bestowed by the earth and sky and realized they could do the same for others. The result was a wilderness program in which he—and later his wife Karen—regularly took teen-agers on eighteen-day treks through the Chihuahuan Desert, where they learned to look to the wind and stars and land and see their own souls.

For him, no more fitting locale for a home could have existed than the grassy slopes of an oak- and piñon-studded peak in the Davis Mountains, Texas's second-highest range. Overlooking forested Skillman Grove and a valley once trod by Apache warriors and westward-bound emigrants, the site would offer him the seclusion he needed to train his falcons, teach them to hunt and kill and return upon command. He was later to wonder whether, there in that mountain shrine, another might be awaiting the opportunity to train *him*.

Karen, a teacher, did not share Forrest's spartan background, but she came to the house as one more finely attuned to the spirit world, if such existed. Though raised in church-dominated Abilene, she eschewed standard Christian doctrines, delving instead into karma, the Hindu belief that a person's every action helps determine the state of his life in his next reincarnation. In fact, Karen already believed she had experienced a close encounter with the spirit world in the home of her widowed grandmother.

Since her grandfather's death, storage rooms along each side of a long, rayless corridor had been kept locked against the past and its memories. Down that hallway walked Karen, her footsteps reverberating on hardwood floor like coffin lids thudding shut. She neared one threshold—and the doorknob turned. She shuddered, felt a chill creep down her spine, and hurried onward. Looking down the shadowy corridor, she saw every other doorknob turn as though triggered by her presence.

She turned and fled screaming.

It was not so surprising to her, then, when the Indian began to disclose his presence in their Davis Mountains home. He revealed himself not only visually during her half-conscious state, but by audible and olfactory modes as well. But the most dramatic indications of intrusion from a world transcending the Keefes' involved psychokinesis: the moving of objects without the use of physical means.

They lay in bed, and the stillness of the night suddenly gave way to the slam of a door, and then a second, a third. Forrest and Karen became alert, listening. It was only the wind, they said. Just the mountain air moaning through the canyon, sweeping through the screens. But the windows—hadn't they left them closed against the chill of winter?

47
The Davis Mountains Spirit

Forrest arose to walk the carpeted hallway, check the spare bedrooms, the closets, the kitchen. He found only the midnight solitude of a mountain hideaway.

That serenity was not destined to continue, as night after night, doors opened, closed, banged. Karen grew afraid of her own home. On a couple of occasions she even wanted to go to a motel. The first few times, Forrest investigated, but not only could he find nothing unusual, he was not even able to determine which doors were involved.

They decided to find out. On the door to a room in which Forrest stored Indian artifacts and wilderness equipment, he hung a deer antler. On the other spare bedroom door, Karen placed a bell. Thereafter, a noise like the clashing of buck deer sometimes accompanied the night sounds—and the Keefes began to pay the small storeroom more attention.

Inside, they began to notice other evidences of psycho-kinesis—but always after the fact. Indian artifacts hanging on the wall turned up on the floor, resting at an angle against the wall—not as if the result of a fall, but as though they had been *placed* there. Rifles, a hunting bow, broadhead arrows, traps, a fishing rod—all at one time or another were found shuffled about as if someone had "just played with them and set them down wherever," Forrest would describe the scene.

At first, Forrest thought Karen had tampered with the objects and Karen believed her husband had. When they found out differently, they reassessed their entire interpretation of the sounds of the night.

Almost by the day, evidence mounted that the house or area held unusual properties. The Keefes left their Doberman pinscher Tonga and a cat inside locked doors and windows one night, and when morning came, the pets were outside—and the house was still locked. It was confusing, prompting the Keefes to question their own memories. When it happened a second time, it became inexplicable.

The Keefes soon began to suspect that the pets were developing a unique relationship with some unseen entity. Not only were the animals released to the vast mountain outdoors at night, but sometimes, lying on the carpet, they would move their heads simultaneously as if watching something beyond human senses cross the room.

But the relationship—if it existed—wasn't always affable. Once, Karen was in the artifact room when the cat squalled, bolted with bristled hair from the closet, and leaped behind a footlocker as though pursued. Thereafter, it shunned both closet and room, which the Keefes came to regard as the center of supernatural activity.

Tonga exhibited similar behavior. Sometimes as the Keefes would walk her down the hallway toward the room, she suddenly would stop and refuse to go further. At times, she even appeared to have been scolded, but not by the hand of Forrest or Karen.

"I think," Forrest told his wife one day, "the dog thinks there's three of us here instead of two."

Before long, he did as well.

Meanwhile, evidence of psychokinesis spread to other areas of the house. Karen, planning to refinish three kitchen chairs, removed the red leather cushions. But a delay in the project saw her replace the seats without bolting, so that they only rested on the frames. One morning the Keefes awoke to discover each of the cushions perfectly in place—only upside down.

A few weeks afterward, a motor belt on the vacuum cleaner snapped as Karen cleaned the carpet. She measured the item, tossed it in the garbage, and at a later date, sent Forrest into Fort Davis to find a replacement. When he returned empty-handed, she drove into town herself and came back with rubber bands she hoped to substitute. Pulling the vacuum cleaner off the top shelf of a closet, she discovered a new belt already in place.

But it was not until the voice came that they began to be convinced. They were in the kitchen, and the rays of the afternoon sun danced across the rocky slope beyond the sink window. And somewhere in that indefinable region between thought and auditory sense, they heard someone humming.

It was not the droning of an electrical appliance, for it carried a human-like melody. And yet the radio was off, no television was playing, and the nearest neighbors were hundreds of yards away. Forrest subsequently would describe it as "faint," but not as though it came from a great distance. It was almost, the Keefes would say, as if it came from within their own minds—the same mode by which the beating of drums later would reach Karen's consciousness.

But the odors which began to sweep through the artifact room were more definitive. Almost perfume-like, they were fleeting: a whiff here, a breath there, and then they would be gone. It was, Forrest later would reflect, as though some invisible presence were passing by.

Several weeks had elapsed now since that first howl in the night, and the cumulative evidence for preternatural phenomena was staggering. "I don't believe in ghosts—never have," Forrest told Karen one night. "I mean, I just don't. But then this started happening and"—he laughed nervously—"*something*. I can't explain what it is. The way I've educated myself is biologically. I'm not religious—at all. But if you don't believe in a devil or a god or anything, it seems to me it wouldn't affect me. I've been scared to death a lot of times before and have always been able to find out what it was that scared me. Well, this time I can't figure it out. You try to just rationalize it all and after a while you can't. All this suddenly is here, and you just accept it."

But to what did it all bear testimony?

The Keefes looked at the esoteric events occurring about them and then at the ancient homeland of the Apache in the canyons below, and with a war cry the mountains screamed the answer.

Indian! Spirit! Specter!

Subsequent research supported their deduction. An anthropology work revealed that warriors braided aromatic sweet grass in their locks, dabbed themselves with musk. Further study uncovered the fact that Highway 166, winding through ridgebacks and oaks half a mile away, followed the route of a one-time war trail.

But to the Keefes, the most persuasive evidence would come seemingly from the presence itself.

An avid collector of Indian artifacts, Forrest thoroughly had searched the small peak on which their home rested. But while arrowheads and scrapers were common elsewhere in these mountains, this particular plat was strangely void of archaeological finds. It was almost as if warriors had shunned this ground, holding it in fear, safeguarding it as sacred.

They sat in the living room that night: Karen, her mother, her father. Earlier, as darkness had crept across the cacti and boulders, the Keefes had detailed the cryptic events, stressed that the entity's characteristics and obsessions suggested an Indian origin. Now, as Forrest showered, something suddenly slammed against the front door and began scratching.

Three persons stiffened, exchanged glances, laughed nervously. The cat had since taken sick and died and Tonga was in a back bedroom. What other explanation could there be? They went to the door, flipped on the outside light, saw nothing. And heard only the nocturnal air softly moaning through the mountains.

They stayed inside, dismissing it as just another in a long line of unusual nights.

The next morning, Forrest found it at the bottom of the front steps: a flint scraper. Pink. White. Perfectly preserved from the day on which an Indian last had used it to grate the hide of an animal. To the Keefes, it was the seal of confirmation put on their threshold by the entity itself—and Karen's fear became full-blown.

She would be in a back bedroom or hallway, and forebodings suddenly would raise bumps on her flesh, lift the hair on her neck. Uncanny terror would send her fleeing, screaming for Forrest as she ran. She began to avoid the artifact room, especially when darkness reigned. "I don't like to spend any time in there by myself when it's dark," she told Forrest. "It scares me. It's fear of the unknown. I keep wondering—since it obviously has the capacity to open doors, turn knobs—whether or not at some point he would pick up a knife, hurt you."

But Forrest, once regarded as a sorcerer by his Mexican neighbors in McAllen because of his intimacy with wildlife, looked into his own background and began to feel a bizarre oneness with the entity.

"I can't figure this out, but this doesn't scare me," he told her. "It likes the dog, it likes my room, it likes my stuff. If it is a spirit of some kind, I'm pretty convinced it's an Indian, a man, just one of them. It's like a common interest or something. Indians—I like what they do. It's not a threat. I'd like the thing just to appear, sit there in the chair and talk—maybe it knows something I don't—but it won't do it."

Gradually, the couple came to regard something other than the house as the specific domain of the spirit. There were the tiny buddhas on the window sill and Indian points to appraise, while an almost demonic quality seemed to lurk in the ornamental wall hanging of a dragon. "It resides," Karen said one evening only half-jokingly, "in that wall hanging."

But taking all into consideration, they saw in the small peak itself that of which wraiths are made.

"It's as if someone's walking up and down through here," Karen suggested one night, "as if someone put this house in the way of where *they* used to walk."

"It doesn't try to run us out," said Forrest. "It's like the house is set down on a pathway. It goes through the house, or sometimes it'll hang out. Sometimes I guess it'll choose to go around the house."

Nevertheless, eerie activity within the house intensified and became corroborated by others. With the Keefes away, Jim Hayman of High Frontier brought a group of teen-agers out. They were watching television in the dining-kitchen area when the light above the sink went black, only to be replaced moments later by brilliance. It was a cycle which would be repeated throughout the evening, and when Jim later told the Keefes, they informed him it never had occurred before.

Nor did it afterward.

Spring enveloped the Big Bend with a rainbow of cactus blooms, and while the Keefes led teen-agers into the backcountry, High Frontier administrative supervisor John Ryan stayed in their home. He was not destined to sleep well. Wary against possible entry by illegal aliens, he was always careful to lock the house before retiring. And yet, one black night he was awakened by the slamming of windows and doors. He arose and walked the hallway to discover both outside doors open—and no one around.

That is, no one *human*.

John remained at the Keefes' another two and a half weeks, and every fourth or fifth night the event would be repeated. He would be awakened or rise at dawn; the doors would be ajar. "I'd know for a fact," he would say later, "these doors were closed when I went to bed. A couple of nights there was wind out, but the front door is a tight fit and it was just impossible for the wind to open it. A couple of times I'd be up in early evening and twenty- to thirty-mile-per-hour gusts would be coming through, and it wouldn't open them up."

But what in the name of Heaven had?

"There was just nothing there," he would reflect. "The dog never acted unfriendly toward anybody or any thing."

That *thing* was to make itself known to John before his stay was over: He slept in the master bedroom that night; the full moon splashed the mountainsides with twilight. He was a light sleeper; when he stayed at High Frontier, kids merely could approach his door and he would become fully conscious. But he was alone now, in total isolation. Or so he believed.

He awoke suddenly. It was four a.m. The room was dark, and still. And no longer, he realized, occupied only by himself.

Later, he would be at a loss to describe the sensation.

"There was some kind of presence, some other type of entity," he would mutter. "Something just walked through that door and

I woke up. I knew someone was in there, walking through the bedroom. But there wasn't anything around."

It stirred John's blood, not curdled it, but he stayed awake the rest of the night trying to decipher the mystery. He couldn't.

When the Keefes returned, dwelling on the theory their home might rest on an ancient pathway or burial ground, footsteps began to shatter the nocturnal stillness as though in response.

Blam! Blam, blam, blam! Thunderous. One after another. From the hallway outside their bedroom. At all hours of the night.

When it first occurred, Karen urged Forrest to investigate, determine if Tonga were responsible. He would find her soundly asleep on a sofa—and no other logical possibility existed.

They but accepted it, though with confusion.

"It waits," reflected Karen, "until we go in our bedroom and shut the door, and it never opens that door."

"Or bangs on it either," added Forrest.

But no other door was to escape unscathed the night they returned from Lincoln National Forest in New Mexico. Forrest was to remember that black hour as one of the two most vivid encounters they would have with the entity, and for Karen, it would be another in a succession of terrifying episodes.

It was three-thirty in the morning. They slept soundly as darkness blanketed the mountainside in tranquility. And then suddenly they were startled into awareness to face gloom that held hostility.

Throughout the house, doors had begun to slam savagely. They slammed and banged and thundered and vibrated the walls, utter bedlam replacing harmony.

Forrest and Karen lay there and listened in awe. "We came back and it's like we made it mad," said Forrest. "I'm tired of checking things out—there's just never anything there."

The maelstrom became stillness, but a second graphic encounter was yet to come: Again, the sun already had plunged behind the western peaks. But this time Forrest was awake; he sat writing a letter at the table. The overhead light flooding the dining-kitchen area created a vivid contrast between the lucency of the secured back door and the blackness of the sink window. And then the outside storm door began to rattle.

Forrest glanced over at it, tried to ignore it. The dog was outside, he told himself, that's all it was.

But it persisted, surging in volume from a clatter to a roar to a crashing fortissimo, magnifying in intensity from a vibration to a tremor to an earth-wrenching convulsion.

"It got louder and louder and louder," he would say later, "until it was so loud it was crazy."

He rushed to the door, reached for the knob. The moment his fingers touched it, only silence reigned.

He flung the door open, looked out into the night, shouted the dog's name. From far up the slope came her answering bark.

He took the storm door in his hands, tried to recreate the upheaval he had heard by shaking it with all his strength—and it barely gave. He had stood there a few inches away from the mad quaking, and yet he could not explain it. It had been—in a word— "crazy."

Late June brought with it the first showers of summer, painting the mountainsides with greenery. Almost six months had passed since the bungalow first had served as their honeymoon cottage, and now they cast their eyes beyond the bastion of Mitre Peak and Twin Mountains to the south to their own wilderness retreat a few miles from Alpine. There, a home that truly would be theirs was rising, timber by timber, from a mountain valley.

It was time to leave the bungalow—and its entity. They crated their belongings, boxed up the dragon and tiny buddhas, gathered the items from the artifact room.

And took one last look around.

It had been a puzzling stay, a half-year without explanation. But owner Rod Crowder never had experienced anything unusual at the house, though he was yet to spend a night within its doors. Neither had the previous tenants, Joe and Dorothy Nigrelli, encountered the supernatural. But they had noticed peculiar odors, and from their new home a quarter-mile away, they had seen a strange flickering light crawling along the mountain slope.

Karen had no regrets at moving. She had feared the presence for a long while. But Forrest's relationship with the entity had deepened, reaching a point at which he had come to regard it as his own otherworldly soul-mate.

This man so entwined with creation stood in the living room and surveyed a final time the hallway, doors, chairs, remembering all, and a twinge of sadness filled his eyes.

"It never bothered me," he reflected quietly. "It's not a harmful thing, not a real profound type of haunting. Anything that existed that long ago, lived out its life in the wilderness, would have advanced knowledge. If you could get an Indian back from the 1800s and just have him around and could communicate with him, it would be priceless."

He paused, as though flooded by an image of a falcon soaring into the sky, blending with all that was free and natural. "The Indians, they believed birds of prey—*everything*—was part of the spiritual. Here, it was like having a spiritual friend. Why it came here, I don't know. It may have come the day we came."

He looked at Karen, and a serenity seemed to envelop the house. "I hope," he said softly, "it goes with us."

And from the artifact room came only silence.

PART 2

Backcountry

Big Bend Ranch

In the heart of the crags, gorges, and gnarled tablelands that compose most of Big Bend Ranch in southeastern Presidio County lies a wilderness oasis.

Here, water cascades over a precipice, sprays a mist in the air as it tumbles down to create a double stream shaped like a diamond against the rock face of the "Pedestal." A tranquil pool awaits it below, its peaceful ripples shaded by cottonwoods, willows, and oaks entwined by maidenhair fern and grapevines, lending credence to its description by some as a "West Texas Eden."

Madrid Falls is that, and more, for in the desert, water means life, and hope does not exist apart from it. And beyond the falls' hermitage in Chorro Canyon—which winds westward for a mile from the arroyo of Fresno Canyon—and throughout the remaining 326,000 acres of backcountry seared by the Big Bend sun, lies nothing but arid desolation.

With 255,000 acres now controlled by the State of Texas as a state natural area, Big Bend Ranch owes its genesis to hardy pioneers—call them Howard and Bogel and Fowlkes, among others—who challenged the Chihuahuan Desert and hewed from it a ranch sprawling and mysterious. Those stalwarts have now passed from the scene, but the land and its rugged charm continue to lure others, among them John L. Guldemann, last foreman of the ranch and first superintendent of the natural area.

"The appeal of Big Bend Ranch is the vast expanse of land," said Guldemann, who cowboyed on the spread from 1979 until its acquisition by the state in 1988. "[It's] the solitude, the ability to ride across it horseback to view it, to enjoy the western way of life. You get quite a feeling of freedom and uninhibitedness, to be able

Rugged Cañon Leon in Big Bend Ranch opens up to a mountain wall. (Courtesy John L. Guldemann)

to get up and go out and look in all directions and not have to worry about running into anybody or bumping into anything."

Indeed, Big Bend Ranch has been variously described as either remote, scenic, and an enormous asset for future generations, or worthless. Add to those, "desolation incarnate," as many of the persons who have flown its expanses, jeeped its roads, hiked its trails, will attest.

On a desert flat thirty-four miles from pavement lies old ranch headquarters—Sauceda, it is known locally—a white, Spanish-style bungalow. Its walls are fortress-like, insulation against the awesome heat which sometimes crests near one hundred twenty degrees. With an outdoor patio and lengthy, covered porch, the house occupies a lonely setting, with ridges hugging the eastern horizon and desert sweeping toward the setting sun. And yet the vast ruggedness cradling it gives companionship of its own. For this is the land of self-discovery, where every step toward death in the desert is a step deeper into the immense universe of enigma indwelling every man. Civilization is a memory, the struggle for survival an ever-present obsession.

And mystery reigns unbridled, even when logic demands it shouldn't. For example, cited Guldemann, Sauceda may harbor some wayward spirit, doomed to haunt the night in some inexplicable quest.

"We had a ghost down here at headquarters," he related. "Sometimes we've heard—late at night—somebody banging on the anvil in the saddle house, just making a helluva racket. You'd go out there and there's nobody there."

Beyond Sauceda, those who seek the land's secrets often must take to four-wheel-drive vehicles, horses, or hiking boots. Even in latter ranching days, cowboys in southern Fresno Canyon had to rely almost solely on saddle stock for transportation, and where horse paths ended, foot trails took over.

As in the Solitario.

If ever a mountain range were aptly named ("Solitaire" or "Hermit"), it is this eight-mile-wide island of loneliness rising 2,000 feet from a desert ocean to a summit elevation of 5,131 feet at Fresno Peak. But it is a wasteland rising out of wasteland, devoid of the life-sustaining qualities inherent in many ranges. Ravaged by the highest evaporation rate in Texas, its barrens are scarred by bluffs and gullies that give no hint of life other than in *tinajas*—rock pockets which collect water after infrequent rains.

The massive peaks that form the bizarrely symmetrical perimeter are curled upward like the pages of a burning book. From an aircraft at 10,000 feet, it appears as though a giant hand has wrenched countryside, ripped it apart, and flung it back again. The lower "shutup" is a V-shaped gash 750 feet deep through its outer battlement, providing access to the battered interior only by jeep road or trail.

One's initial impression is that the Solitario is either the result of a collision of the Earth with a gargantuan meteorite or the remnant of a volcano, for it seems unnatural to the terrain, standing aloof from the desert formations and lesser mountains that fringe it. Geologists, indeed, point to a volcanic origin, but see here, as well, evidence of a cataclysmic upthrust, and to view it is to acknowledge that nothing short of cataclysm could have contorted mountains so and twisted peak after peak at the same angle.

While night in the Solitario brings respite from the heat, it may also harbor great danger and mystery. Guldemann, who worked cattle in the Solitario every July and August, considered the range both "unique" and "scary" because of the bizarre characteristics of lightning in its confines.

"I don't know if it was the composition of the rock or whatever, but lightning would start flashing [all around] at night and it would be terrifying to all of the men," he recalled.

Beyond nature's display of sovereignty are the rumored preternatural occurrences in the Solitario. Build a campfire there, and a stranger suddenly may be sharing it—only to vanish into the darkness as quickly as he appeared.

But that spirit is not alone in this land of enigma. Below the Solitario, near the old Harry Smith house built in Fresno Canyon in 1918, a white-gowned woman is said to walk the night. "There's something down there, so nobody wants to stay down there," noted Julia Tredaway, wife of the one-time ranch foreman.

"It may be old woman Smith," said her husband Marion Tredaway, passing along local folklore. "Her husband left the country after she died."

Elsewhere on the ranch, restless spirits are said to reveal themselves by modes other than visual. "We used to have a trapper here named Juan Salazar," related Guldemann. "He was a [water] pipeline rider at the time. And he came in one afternoon [and] he had a tow sack full of bones. And we asked him where he got the bones. And he said for the last couple of weeks he'd been riding by this little shallow, dug-out cave on his way home from the pipeline; every time he'd go by, he'd hear somebody whisper, 'Juan! Juan!' But this day he'd been working on the pipeline and he had a shovel, and he stopped and dug in that cave and dug up the remains of several people."

Too, Big Bend Ranch is said to harbor buried treasures, among them a large cache of Pancho Villa's rifles. Moreover, the spirits of the long-departed often are enmeshed with such legends. In the Mexicano Creek drainage, for example, ghosts supposedly are charged with guarding stashed Spanish gold.

No one knows the purpose, however, of the ghost fires that torch the night in at least two areas of the ranch. In the 5,135-foot Bofecillos Mountains, many reports have filtered down, from the 1920s and before, of spirit apparitions, ghost bells and bizarre lights. Meanwhile, where the 5,223-foot Cienega Mountains loom over Cienega Camp away up toward Shafter, cowboys staying into the dark have witnessed a mysterious light for years.

"It's just a ghost light that sits there in a place [where] there's just no inhabitants," noted Guldemann, who observed the light on numerous occasions. "It's sort of an orange-white light. There's no movement to it. You're looking southwest; it appears to be just maybe a matter of six, seven miles [away] at most. There's no explanation why there should be a light there; the closest ranch would be tens and twenties of miles away."

The Cienega ghost fire has been joined, on occasion, by other lights in the night sky above Cienega Camp. When Guldemann and his wife Keri were living at the site in 1986, dusk found friends departing their home in a Jeep Wagoneer. The next morning, Guldemann answered the telephone to hear a chilling story related by the driver.

"As they drove out, they entered a big mesquite thicket not a half-mile from the house," narrated Guldemann. "They turned a corner and the headlights flashed toward a ship, as big as two or

63

three Greyhound buses or bigger. It was just hovering silently right above the tree line. He said he couldn't tell whether it was white with red lights or red with white lights.

"He jumped out of the Wagoneer and started going for it, and he said it sounded like about four jets just took off and the thing just started rising out of sight. And before he could get back in his vehicle and drive out to higher ground, it was out of sight."

After hearing the account, Guldemann followed the tracks of the Wagoneer to the location. "The ground was soft enough that you could see where he—at the curve—had made a radical left, a stop, and jumped out of his car," said Guldemann. "His cap was on the ground there and the knob off his gear shift lever."

Though the Guldemanns had neither seen nor heard anything strange the prior evening, soon afterward an unusual noise lured Keri out into the dark, where she watched a mysterious object streak the sky.

Less sphinx-like than unidentified flying objects and ghosts, but just as awe-inspiring in its elemental way, is Colorado Canyon, away to the south, where the Rio Grande at 2,400 feet slashes through mountains. White water sweeps over boulders, crashes against 800-foot rock walls. River runners flock here in spring and autumn, sometimes claiming the rapids are consistently faster, the experience more sensual, than even in Big Bend National Park's Santa Elena Canyon forty miles downstream. *Camino del Rio*, a highway praised nationally for its course through such ruggedly beautiful country, follows the snaking river to the mouth of the canyon, then veers away to skirt it again several miles downstream.

Midway through the gorge, a crevice called Closed Canyon cleaves a mountain as though by gigantic saber. No more than a few yards wide, the rift bears the robes of grandeur, as do many of the side canyons along the twenty-eight mile stretch of river which serves as the southern boundary of the ranch and nation.

An irony exists here, for the water which has made such an impact on the topography has not even dented the sovereignty of the Chihuahuan Desert. Only a few feet beyond the carrizo, salt cedar, and seep willow which crowd the river bank, wasteland with creosote and sotol again reigns supreme. It remains unchallenged throughout Big Bend Ranch except in that oasis that lies hidden in remote Chorro Canyon several hours by four-by-four vehicle and trail from the nearest improved road.

Tires slip and grate rubble in descending into Fresno Canyon, a mile-wide valley separating the Solitario from the Bofecillos. Along its floor lie occasional signs of one-time Indian habitation—pictographs, grinding stones, arrowheads. Low, brushy trees infest portions of the dry arroyo, then thicken before a solitary spring along a hillside.

At the mouth of Chorro Canyon, the jeep becomes useless. The passengers don hiking boots and seek an ill-defined trail, which winds westward through cottonwoods and oaks. The trickle of running water gradually intensifies until it echoes between narrowing gorge walls. The trail disappears, mossy rock replacing it. A stream surfaces to cascade over a thirty-foot bluff. Fifty yards further, the upper falls suddenly appear through the greenery of willows and ferns, a streak of white in the morning sunlight plummeting one hundred feet into the sheltered pool frequented by the Madrean cliff frog and its relative, the canyon tree frog.

Moisture. Coolness. Life. The splash of water against water testifies that here the three exist as one.

Above the rim, one hundred vertical feet away, the desert unfurls into the distance.

And from there comes only the silence of utter devastation and the haunting summons of the land's spirits.

The author on the crest of the rugged west escarpment of the Guadalupe Mountains.

Soloing the Guadalupes

*D*ay One: Darkness crawls upward along the crags of the Guadalupe Mountains to skirt gorge and wash, blanket pinnacle and spire, until even the upper forested slopes are but silhouettes against a sky jeweled with stars.

Dust clings to the laces of a single pair of hiking boots slashing up ridge; the waffled soles, grinding against rubble, flank bluff or precipice either to the left or right, decreed solely by the switchbacks which snake along the northern wall of Pine Canyon.

Behind and below, the drive-in campground at 5,695 feet retreats, disappears into the shadows beyond jutting slags, sheer cliffs. And overhead, the awesome fortress of the Guads looms more than 8,000 feet above sea level, a full mile above the northern reaches of the Chihuahuan Desert.

A pair of boots. Seven quarts of water. Fifty-four pounds of food and equipment. And I, a lone hiker confronting a vast, rugged wilderness of arid mountains, gutted by canyons, blanketed by forests, scalded by the swollen sun.

Solo.

It will be more than two and a half days before I will see another human being again, and before I do I will have scaled 8,700 feet of mountainside, plummeted into gaping canyons and climbed out again a dozen times, and thirty miles of trail will have savaged my hiking boots, dragged my pack downward against saddle-sore shoulders, rotated me skewer-like to fiery rays that broil cheeks and neck a deep scarlet.

Day Two: I unshoulder my pack at the wooded summit of Bush Mountain, at 8,676 feet the second-highest peak in Texas. I rub the tendons that run downward from my neck, inspect the blisters that have gnawed into my heels. I walk to the boulders at the edge of the precipice, my boots pausing a foot from the rim, and stare down a vertical mile at canyon, gully, gray wasteland splashed white by dry salt beds in almost symmetrical fashion.

I am alone, but the heights offer their own companionship, the forest of ponderosa pine at my shoulder providing solace in the face of the stark desert ravaged by the same blazing sun that brings the taste of my sweat to my lips.

Day Three—Morning: As my heart hammers against my rib cage, I stop to rest aching feet, knotted muscles, beneath a shady ponderosa pine hugging the western escarpment along Cox Tank Trail. The countryside is a purplish blur 5,000 feet beneath me, while forty-five miles distant, the twin peaks of the Cornudas rise against the horizon like errant strokes of an artist's brush. And but for the neatly squared sections of green carved into the desert twenty miles away by the irrigated fields of Dell City, no signs exist in one hundred miles of territory that man ever has trodden this land.

I am in the deep backcountry now of one of America's most remote national parks, as enmeshed in solitude and as far from civilization as twentieth-century man can be. I am two days by trail from the nearest person, and on this day my closest and most guarded companion is the quart canteen of water that rides at my hip. I am several hours away from the base camp I established at Blue Ridge at 8,200 feet, and before I can return I must descend 2,000 feet into West Dog Canyon and then scale the distance in a ten-mile loop.

To lose my canteen, to run short of water, is to leave myself subjected to the strength-sapping rays of the sun, a loss of vital body fluids and minerals, with no natural water source available to replenish them.

For in the Guads, water is life.

Day Three—Midafternoon: I am down to less than a cup of water. I have underestimated the demands of the day hike. The sun is a scorching ninety-five degrees, and I must traverse a treeless trail up a 2,000-foot climb, survive five hours more. I think to myself, "I am alone. I make it, or I die." I know I am right. In this, the most isolated portion of Guadalupe Mountains National Park, days may pass before another hiker comes along. I think about the three quarts of water at base camp. I hope I do not sprain an ankle, twist a knee, anger a rattler. I have only myself to depend on. I am satisfied.

Day Three—Late Evening: Base camp. Water. Food. I collapse inside my nylon tent, savor the taste of liquid running down inside me. Turkeys gobble from outside. A deer's hooves clomp past. I am tired. But no longer alone. I have the forest about me, three quarts of water beside my sleeping bag. The wind blows savagely that night, flapping the tent and moaning through ponderosa pine and Douglas fir, but I do not awaken. For there is tranquility.

Day Four: I grasp overhead megaliths, pull myself to the summit of 8,362-foot Hunter Peak, sprawl across the boulder-strewn crest as the sun is blinding incandescence in my eyes. The wind is strong here, tugging at my collar, and two birds ride the currents, swish by my head. The world recedes from me, sweeping into the distance, plunging into the depths. The Bowl of the Guads to the north, its alpine-forested slopes a carpet of green. Pine Canyon a half-mile gash at my knees. The gnarled slopes of Guadalupe Peak, Shumard, Bartlett a battlement beyond. And a hundred miles of utter desolation unfurling like a choppy sea to the east. And still no evidence but that I am the only person in the world.

In three hours I will have descended 2,700 feet of craggy mountainside, sought the ample water supply at Pine Springs ranger station, felt pavement rather than boulders against my feet, heard the blare of car horns and the roar of diesel trucks, tasted the gasoline fumes that hang in the air along Highway 62-180, again sampled all the refinements of civilization.

But for now, there is only I, and the mountains rising before me, the canyons yawning beneath me, the forest urging me into the backcountry again.

And I am at peace.

Big Bend Adventurer

❀

*H*e went into the backcountry alone, on foot, carrying only water, cheese, prunes, poncho, and machete, and stayed days at a time.

It was the mid-1930s. Big Bend's mist-shrouded peaks, parched lowlands, yawning canyons, and sheer precipices were so remote that only wagon roads gave passage, and beyond them lay only utter desolation. It was here, in league with two hundred eighty other young men in the Civilian Conservation Corps, that he lived almost three years, first in a tent and then in a primitive wooden structure.

He would follow game trails up into the forested slopes of the Chisos Mountains, through boulder-clogged gullies of the desert floor, between jagged walls of canyons which gutted barren crags broiled by the swollen sun. Game trails meant wildlife, eking out an existence in a seemingly dry world. They also meant water. And water, in this isolated frontier hardly touched by man, meant survival.

More than half a century later, James Owens still stood unyielding to nature, and continued to hearken to the primeval drumbeat of all that is wild and free.

In no other locale in the Pecos frontier are those qualities displayed so vividly as in the great bend of the Rio Grande. Occasionally unearthly, often weird, always intoxicating, that vast region within the Chihuahuan Desert held an almost mystical bond with him.

"The Big Bend intrigues me to no end," he said, relaxing in his Midland residence as various wilderness portraits stared down at him: Santa Elena Canyon, Blue Creek, the South Rim of the Chisos. His hair was snowy, thinning, but the scarcity of wrinkles

James Owens outfitted for the backcountry.

in his features belied his years. "I like the feeling of going somewhere where not a lot of people are going. It gives me personal satisfaction. I can feel just terrible, and I can go up in the backcountry—I may not see anybody for a week—and when I come back I've got myself together."

Such quests for self-discovery in what is now Big Bend National Park brought him into intimate kinship with topographic features perhaps undiscovered even by the National Park Service. For in crisscrossing the wilderness in the 1930s few sites failed to record his bootprints.

He was twenty years old, and the nation was fighting a brutal depression. He joined the CCC, a federal program which took youths off the streets and rails, provided them with jobs, food, and medical attention. The CCC largely was responsible for the development of several state parks, and Owens first helped construct facilities at Lampasas State Park before transferring to Big Bend State Park (now Big Bend National Park) in May 1934.

As a CCC member, he received thirty-four dollars a month—twenty-five of which went directly to his family. Later he would be promoted to the forty-five dollar-a-month position of "local experience man" and serve as a clerk to the superintendent.

Slashing a road through a 5,760-foot pass, the CCC set up camp in then-untrampled Chisos Basin, a great hollow cradled by the dominant peaks of the range. Although Owens was a part of the operation, the development of the area saddened him. Once, only the Apaches had ruled here, they and the desert sun and animals as free as the wind. Then had come the ranchers with their goats and cattle. And now, true "civilization" finally had invaded.

But at the same time that Owens was witnessing the cruel hand of man against nature, he was becoming more and more a part of that nature, sensing within him the dawning of an inexplicable oneness with it.

"Whenever I get in that country I just become a part of it—my soul blends in with it," he would reflect, groping to explain a feeling that transcended words. "To me, it's natural. I worship, in a sense, nature, because it's God's creation, because it's a part of me. I'm a part of the universe; I'm a part of the cosmos. You don't separate the physical from the spiritual—it's a blend."

It was a union which fostered exhilaration and danger in Owens's CCC days, as his adventures became legion. They carried him to the Rio Grande, where he challenged the waters which sluice through the awesome twelve-mile gash known as Santa Elena Canyon. This snaking rift in the Mesa de Anguila always has imparted to man a sense of his own insignificance, ever since a topographical boating expedition in 1899 reported that by extending oars toward the 1,500-foot walls "we could almost touch either."

Once inside, where the ebony fortifications squeeze close and the sky is a narrow shaft of brightness far above, crafts are entombed to surge inexorably downstream. There is no turning back against the pull of wicked rapids, no scaling the vertical battlements, no escaping except by letting the wall-to-wall water sweep the vessels to its end. In the midst of the canyon lies Rock Slide, a quarter-mile stretch of white spray and deadly undercurrents spawned by the war between river and great boulders loathe to let it flow. Some who have dared its rapids even in sophisticated rubber rafts have been sucked fatally to the depths, yet Owens and his four companions sported only truck inner tubes.

Stars still studded the morning sky as they put in upstream at the adobe village of Lajitas. Six brutal hours later, their primitive crafts churned into the vertical slit that marked the canyon's mouth. Inside, waters savaged inner tubes and men alike. Undertows and maelstroms tried to claim them, suck them under, but the men paddled free only to face equally dangerous river dynamics around the next bend. When a great roar told them Rock Slide loomed just ahead, they attained the Mexican bank, portaged up and over the boulders that clung to the wall. And later, when the current subsided, they could do nothing but swim the final four miles out of the canyon.

Having found such excitement in the depths of a gorge, Owens later sought to heighten his adventure by clawing to the sky. Hiking solo one day, he tried to scale a brutally exposed portion of Ward Mountain where lichen made every move precarious.

A sudden downpour drenched him, leaving the precipice slippery, the handholds impossible. He clung to a crevice for two hours, waiting for the rain to stop, the sun to dry the mossy cliff so he could descend.

He survived—but it taught him a lesson. Never again would he intentionally take that one extra step beyond his limitations.

"I like to take a chance," he would reflect later, "but I like to take a *calculated* chance. Foolishly brave people don't live long."

With that philosophy, he continued his assaults on the barrens. A high-ranking Mexican official came to the area to explore the possibility of establishing a Mexican national park directly across the Rio Grande from the Big Bend. Owens accompanied him deep into the alpine forest of the Sierra Fronteriza, an igneous extrusion that dwarfs the Chisos, and they burst upon a sparkling lake so clear that Owens could see speckled trout "as long as my arm" darting through its "out-of-this-world" waters.

Great riches also passed before his eyes. He stumbled upon a silver mine in Mexico and viewed a vein so broad several fingers couldn't cover it. Silver prices were down; the mine had been abandoned as worthless. Today, it might be worth a fortune.

Several times he tangled with predators in the Chisos, including an episode in which he chased a black bear from a bee hive on 7,835-foot Emory Peak in order to claim its honey for himself. On another occasion he stood outside a cave far up Emory's rocky slope and watched two companions flee from the shadowy depths, a half-grown black bear at their heels. Twice, mountain lions breathed down his neck. Hiking along Blue Creek, he looked up at a rock outcropping at his shoulder to see a great cat's eyes fixed on him. Making his way down the forested slopes of Emory in a later quest, he heard footsteps at his back. Whirling, he saw a mountain lion stalking him.

He learned that the desert sometimes racks the body, plays tricks with the mind. A youngster once vanished; Owens and other volunteers scoured the desert where the sun baked land and skull alike. By the time they found him, the boy had lost forty pounds from dehydration and become so disoriented that he ran from the searchers, sought to lose them. They had to chase him down, bring him to safety by force.

Owens crowded enough adventure into a brief three years to fill most person's lives, and then he "dropped out" of the back-country, taking a thirty-year hiatus from the Big Bend upon quit-ting the CCC in 1936.

But the basic character traits honed by nature continued to rule him. He joined the U.S. Marines in World War II and fought at Iwo Jima. He acquired a bachelor of science degree in animal science from Texas A&M University and later added master's degrees in soil science and biological science. He taught high school voca-tional agriculture and then ascended to the college ranks at Howard College at Big Spring, where he specialized in microbiology, chemistry, anatomy, and ecology of wildlife management.

He also added a wife along the way, and later a pair of daughters whom he once led up Mitre Peak in the Davis Moun-tains.

But all the while, the mystique of the Big Bend continued to haunt him, until finally in 1966 he "came home."

But his return to the wilderness of his youth was bittersweet, tainted by images of pavement, modern structures, and scores of milling people in the Basin where civilization once had been a memory. And too, the razing of ancient huts throughout the park had claimed priceless history.

"It had destroyed what I considered the virginity of the place," he would reflect sadly. "I was down there when the old-timers were there and had seen the flavor of it when it was ranch country with nothing but wagon roads." And then he would fond-ly recount eating supper many nights with pioneer ranchers who had carved out a rough-and-tumble life in this bend where every man had worn a gun, and lore and legend had flowed freely. "They need to save it, keep it for people who are venturesome."

Owens, for one, still fit that description even as a septuage-narian, having found upon retirement that his desire to confront new challenges and conquer them had not waned. Channeling his energies into outdoor photography, he embarked on a quest for portraits of Texas wildlife.

The search led him still further down the path of self-discovery.

Dabbed with skunk scent and outfitted in a camouflage suit that left only his eyes exposed, he huddled within a spiny allthorn bush in the Davis Mountains and waited.

Directly before him perched a mockingbird, unaware that he was anything but shrubbery, while only a couple of feet away a roadrunner stood staring him in the eye.

Owens did not flinch. He couldn't afford to. For approaching the nearby water hole was the object of his days of planning and hours of waiting—an antelope herd.

Clicking off shots of these animals in quick succession as he would other wildlife forms, Owens meshed with their world and achieved a personal satisfaction that seemed almost in the spiritual realm. "Just to sit there and eyeball those things that close—that's where I get my highs," he reflected.

Still, there were other adventures which awaited, including the kind on which true insight is founded. Nearing seventy, he backpacked a forty-mile course through Telephone Canyon in the desolate crags of the Dead Horse Mountains—a fitting appellation. The sun sapped his strength, dehydrated him to the danger point, and the rocks and spiny desert plants carved deep blisters into his heels until every step became agony. But he was isolated, at one with nature, and he was content.

For the experience taught him that, despite the encroachment of civilization, the Big Bend is so vast, so rugged, that man's hand may dent, but nature's sovereignty will abide.

And with it, the soul of a man who "blended in" so inseparably.

Comanche Springs Cave

It is the very fountainhead of the springs where Comanches camped on the War Trail to Mexico and emigrants filled their kegs after struggling through barrens.

Comanche Springs Cave: a maze of water-hewn channels, domes, pits, and squeezes, hidden beneath the city of Fort Stockton and its fabled Comanche Springs.

For millennia that system of springs gushed forth enormous quantities of water—sixty-five million gallons a day during the early years of the twentieth century. It quenched the thirst of wildlife and cowboys and freighters, spawned an army post, gave birth to a city of nine thousand on the fringe of the Chihuahuan Desert. It abided while cacti and creosote waged war for the surrounding alkaline waste, and even decades after the irrigated crops of the farmer stilled the flow, it unleashed new ways to excite the imagination.

And all because three brothers persevered five years to see their innovative quest become reality.

Dennis, Glenn, and Haley Haynes grew up roaming the back-country hills near Sanderson and hearing tales of Comanche Springs. They eventually found in caving a quality that stirred their lifeblood and propelled them into years of exploring the state's sub-terranean features. When Dennis and Glenn moved to Fort Stockton and listened to mysterious stories weaved by water-well drillers (bits plummeting through cavities) and by homeowners (wells pumping dry one day and surging the next), they reached into their background and decided an intricate labyrinth of aque-ous and dry channels lay below.

By then, the Chief Spring—largest in the system—long since had been concealed by Comanche Springs Swimming Pool, which

A chamber deep within Comanche Springs Cave. Taking a respite is Bill Bentley. (Courtesy Ron Jaap)

hovered on stilts like a gigantic bathtub a few feet above the spring and pond bed. Putting their creative vision into action in 1978, they sneaked through locked gates to the underbelly of the pool, studied the standing water in the large crack of the Chief, and discerned a submerged grotto twenty feet inside.

"We could tell it was the tunnel entrance," recalled Dennis, and even in remembrance, the awe of the moment brought a quake to his voice. "We figured it was just rain water that had created a sump, like a trap in a sink. But we didn't think we'd get permission to pump it out [in order to explore it]."

Four and a half frustrating years passed, and still Comanche Springs held fast its secrets. Finally in 1983, with the political prodding of the editor of the *Fort Stockton Pioneer* and a Pecos County commissioner, the spirits smiled on the Haynes brothers and flung them into an adventure where no man had gone before.

A caver rappels down to a pool in Comanche Springs Cave. Checking the rope is Richard Galle. (Courtesy Ron Jaap)

For two straight weeks their combustion-engine pump sucked water from the passageway seemingly to no effect. But their dream remained unclouded, even when they almost were overcome by carbon monoxide fumes that hugged the bottom of the pool.

Ultimately, the pump line began to gurgle, then breathed only air—and before them gaped a forbidding black hole.

Donning headlamps, they descended to the muddy grotto and slithered through 138 feet of squeezeway. An opening suddenly loomed above; they looked to see the beams of their lamps splash into a small chamber that sparkled with thousands of fossilized shells imbedded in limestone for 130 million years.

Their hearts hammering against rib cages, the brothers clawed upward through the mire into the glittering room. And when they placed bootprints before the comparatively dry passage threading onward, they felt they had taken as unparalleled a leap into the chronicles of man as had Neil Armstrong on the moon.

For Dennis, it was an incredible culmination of years of anticipation and wonder.

"The main thing we search for in caving," he reflected later, "is virgin caves. To me, it was like being the first man to cross West Texas . . . or being the first to set foot on the moon. Most people don't understand it, because most people haven't been where no one's been before. It was exciting, not knowing what was around the next curve. You never knew what you were going to find. Comanche Springs is one of the biggest springs in Texas, and we knew it had to be big inside."

With Mary Kay Shannon, curator of Annie Riggs Museum in Fort Stockton, they endured one hundred percent humidity and temperatures in the upper seventies in exploring the maze. They discovered a half-mile of domes and crawlways and "bottomless" pristine pools, which glowed bluish-green before their headlamps. But as they squirmed in and out of the Chief Spring over the days, a problem developed—the rising water table slowly was reclaiming the natural entrance.

With compass, tape measure, and their wits, the cavers decided upon a point in the ceiling of a squeezeway and began to dig their way out. They dug for eight hours, shoveling the dirt back down the doghouse-sized passage. After they had stopped for the night and retreated to the freshness of the air bound only by the starry expanse, Glenn began poking around with a crowbar in a rodent-like hole in the bed of Government Spring—which they believed lay directly above their subterranean dig—and the ground collapsed at his feet.

And for the first time in its millions of years of history, Comanche Springs Cave opened to the hand of man.

Later sealing the cavity against sloughing by inserting six fifty-five-gallon drums welded end-to-end, the cavers abandoned the natural entrance to rising water which soon choked off what had been the sole air vent. Stringing lights for a few hundred feet along the squeezeways where razor-sharp rocks carved into knees and forearms and banged against hard hats, the Haynes brothers began the arduous process of mapping. For each passage and squeeze, each pool and dome, they concocted names: Wounded Knee, Mary's Misery, Stephan's Well. The latter pool stirred their imaginations to a fever pitch, for within its crystal-clear purities gaped a submerged passageway immense enough to accommodate a car. It offered the promise of a much larger cavern system beyond, one that might transcend even their greatest fantasies.

But it was water—the most underrated of all natural forces—that had created Comanche Springs Cave, and water that seemed destined to guard its mysteries forever.

"I think," said a frustrated Dennis, "the cave goes down those wells and comes up to dry space. We think those are big sumps, maybe a quarter-mile long. West of town in Belding they started irrigating in the 1950s and they pumped this spring dry [in the summer of 1951]. So we know if the water was coming all the way to Belding, there's probably ten miles of cave if there's just one tunnel. If it is possible to get into it, we think there's probably one hundred miles of cave in all. We don't think there's any big rooms in it until you get to Belding, where we've had drillers tell us there's ninety- and one hundred-foot cavities."

Most astonishing, he said, the waters may conceal a system that could equal the hundreds of miles of cavern which includes Mammoth Cave in Kentucky. But it was at the whim of those

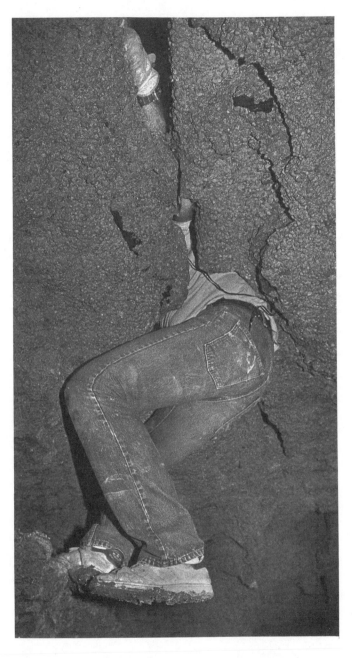

A caver squirms through Mary's Misery in Comanche Springs Cave. (Courtesy Ron Jaap)

waters that man was even given a glimpse inside Comanche Springs Cave, and that same powerful force may ultimately decide to reclaim it entirely. On the first Saturday in October 1986, Comanche Springs began to flow for the first time since 1961. The waters would recede and advance in regular cycle throughout the remainder of the 1980s, with a resulting thirty-foot rise in the cavern's water table by 1990. Many of the already-explored passages again were submerged, and the spring's future as a cavern now rests solely in the inscrutable hands of nature.

Excluding the possibility of an unprecedented drop in the Fort Stockton water table, in only one way may man ever gain the full secrets of Comanche Springs Cave—by scuba diving its mysterious pools and watery channels. Only then might Dennis Haynes's ultimate dream of a vast cavern reach fruition.

Mitre Peak's Might

I clung to the northern battlement of Mitre Peak with five hundred feet of open space at my heels.

I was alone, and above loomed a parapet of sheer rock, while all that separated me from eternity was a two-inch crack into which the toes of my hiking boots were jammed.

Sweat formed silvery beads on my skin, left my aching fingers slippery, unsteady against the fragile handholds. Every muscle in arm and leg was tensed, tiring, quivering under the strain. And tempting me from just one hundred feet above was the summit, silhouetted against the sun as if it were just as unattainable, unyielding, defiant.

Inexperienced, a backpacker a step beyond my element, I could neither climb higher nor skirt the awesome ridge to either side, and I sought the only alternative—retreat. But when I looked down for the cracks that had persuaded me to abandon the security of the jagged six-inch ledge twenty feet below and challenge the wall, I realized too late what the experienced mountaineer always is aware of—the descent is far more demanding and treacherous, for the angles are dizzying, the foot and handholds hidden by the climber's own torso.

To go as far as body and mind will allow, to push oneself to the absolute limits of physical, mental, and emotional endurance so that all logic demands that not another step be taken—and then to take that step—is to *live,* say the wilderness philosophers. It is to enter a realm of consciousness that approaches the metaphysical, where, as though allowed a glimpse beyond an esoteric veil, one is given a chance to tread unexplored territory of the human experience.

And suddenly I knew I had hit that wall of self-limitation and gone beyond, where every step was one deeper into an unknown world. But as I summoned courage for the descent, I wondered if it were to live . . . or to die? For one slip, one moment of dizziness or imbalance, and I would become a part of the mountain forever.

Towering like a pyramid 1,600 feet above a Davis Mountains valley, the peak's gnarled crags and talus slopes resemble a mitre—a pointed headdress worn by Catholic Church hierarchy as a symbol of office. Equating it with a religious object seems fitting, for an old tale of the Big Bend holds that its summit was where Satan first touched Earth upon being cast out of Heaven. Today, *La Mitra* stands alone like a sentinel near Texas Highway 118 midway between Alpine and Fort Davis.

From a distance it is an imposing sight, 6,190 feet of dirt and rock framed against the sky like a misplaced Easter Island monolith. From nearer, the individual spires, volcanic dikes, and weather-smoothed precipices become delineated. Its base is moated by a sea of catclaws which rip and tear flesh, and grotesquely twisted junipers hug rock bluffs and skirt washes.

It is a small Matterhorn without the ice, an obelisk with landslide channels strewn with boulders like bodies on a battleground. A thousand formations—gutted by hollows, cleft by crevices—jut at seemingly impossible angles, lending an alien aura, a surrealistic atmosphere.

The peak grew all the more forbidding on that cold Thanksgiving Day when the clouds descended to swirl about its upper reaches and seize it with tenuous, gray wisps. As a companion and

---

Mitre Peak as viewed from the east.

Mitre Peak's Might

I scrambled up the grassy knoll of tasajillo and rubble, aiming for the hidden palisades above, the icy fog fell upon us, chilled us with a freezing mist that swept down our collars.

Scaling higher through the clouds, we reached great boulders and unearthly columns, standing like contorted tombstones in a Boris Karloff graveyard scene in which fog creeps up from the ground. Below, a silvery sea had drifted across the lowlands, turning lesser ridges and knolls wispy and hiding the valley. Above, visibility was no more than thirty feet, except for fleeting glimpses that revealed precipitous pillars hovering like the embodiment of death with raised scythe.

It was difficult to see through the fog, impossible to determine a route up the escarpment, but easy to imagine the unimaginable, the ordinarily unthinkable. But it was not easy to turn back, to succumb to nature, for I knew that once again the mountain had won, and we had only survived.

The mountain has defeated more than climbers, say geologists: It overcame the crust of the Earth to stand as a monument to its own strength, endurance, and defiance.

Spawned by eruption of a volcano thirty-six million years ago, Mitre Peak is a geologic intrusive, long-since exposed by erosion, according to Dennis Nelson, geology department chairman at Sul Ross State University in Alpine in the 1980s. Mitre's genesis, he said, came when molten rock thrust up through the Earth's crust and crystallized before it reached the surface, forming a buried mountain of igneous rock. Erosion gradually removed the softer dirt and rock from the immediate area, carving out the landscape about the harder geologic matter, until all that remained was 1,600 feet of crystallized magma rising toward the clouds.

Its age, said the geologist, is consistent with other Davis Mountains rocks which have been analyzed with radiometric dating.

Surrounded by evidences of other extensive volcanic activity, including lava flows, or extrusions, Mitre Peak exhibits formations associated with its origin. Along the northern flank protrudes a dike, another exposed intrusive, which probably resulted when magma forced its way into a bedrock fracture caused by the upthrust of the Mitre body. Cavities in boulders may be vesicles, gas bubbles which exploded as the original magma cooled. The sometimes surrealistic spires are a result of the tendency of magma to crystalize in vertical joints, fractured segments, which in turn influence the way the body weathers.

While Nelson noted Mitre's aloofness from the Davis range with which it shares a common heritage—"it does seem to stand alone"—he indicated many intrusive bodies lie in the region. But none can match Mitre Peak for sheer majesty. "Why an intrusive is particularly exposed right there may be a fluke of erosion," he reflected.

Night had fallen along the northern slope of Mitre, and a glacier-like chill swept down from the gnarled spires to crawl inside the dark grotto yawning open to the valley below. The January wind flapped against a plastic raincoat stretched crudely across the opposite opening several yards away, for the house-sized boulder was gutted from one end to the other.

Readjusting ourselves in our sleeping bags against the grotto's ridged rock, we looked down on the boulder-strewn slope and beyond at the valley and plains shadowy in the distance. The moon was phosphorescence through a streaked veil, then the clouds broke and the light cast a soft glow across the lowlands. Simultaneously, the wind died and, from somewhere near, coyotes began to yelp and howl, first in a single voice, then joined by a second and a third, until at last the entire pack wailed its challenge to the sky.

And in the darkness of our primitive shelter, a peace came over us, for the coyotes' song was as beautiful in its own elemental way as any we ever had heard. We later would cherish those memories of serenity and quiet rest, for the next day we were to climb again—and fail.

For other adventurers—those who are aware of and seek the lesser challenge of the southeast face—the summit is attained without incident or danger. It is the traditional route of youngsters from nearby Camp Mitre Peak, a Girl Scout ranch which seems to share a special oneness with the mountain. Not only is each identified with the other by name, but, according to legend, one formation along the slope signifies the Sleeping Maiden, who has in her charge the girls at Camp Mitre.

"As long as girls have been coming here," reflected the camp director, "there's never been a single one injured seriously."

At the summit, Girl Scouts sometimes maintain a registry, perhaps a weather-beaten parchment of names and dates stuffed inside a rusty can. Other climbers have established their own registries, and casual digging in the loose dirt between boulders at the apex may unearth film canisters with hastily scrawled messages. While reflections by mountaineers upon attaining the summits of Himalayan peaks have ranged from the deeply philosophical ("To strive, to seek, to find, And not to yield") to the more practical ("How the heck am I gonna get back down?"), registry comments by amateur climbers who scale Mitre speak wryly of their own insecurities.

"R. David Smith and John P. DeWitt scaled, explored, survived the night on [Mitre]," a climber confidently began an entry. Then the grim reality of the descent to follow subdued his tone. "And *hopefully* descended this same peak July 4-5, Year of our Lord, 1974 A.D."

That the "hopefully" successful descent proved prophetic is denoted by a later entry by the same individual, dated March 30, 1975.

On that blazing July day several years later we were concerned only with making the ascent—we would worry about the plunge down only if it ever proved necessary.

Three times we had confronted the mountain on its own terms—on its north, west, and northwest faces—and three times we had failed. Now, forsaking those routes which demanded experience and climbing equipment, we would skirt the base of the palisades and seek the south wall, which heretofore had been a mystery, hidden behind a mile of mountain.

Beyond the briars that snagged our clothes and savaged our arms and packs, we scrambled up through a narrow chute where wavy grasses and six-foot weeds grew between bordering walls and needles of rock. At its terminus, a thousand feet above the lowlands, we turned to face six hundred feet of boulder piled upon boulder as if by demonic design.

The angles were such that we could see no more than thirty vertical feet above, and once there, no more than another thirty feet. It would be a blind climb, with no way to determine a route beforehand. And the poetic words that delineate the invariable outcome of man's one-on-one confrontation with the unyielding forces of nature seemed to echo from the crags: *The wild must win!*

And slowly, we began to climb, Vibram soles scraping rock, gloved fingers straining to reach cracks. We sought the security of a piñon with twisted limbs reaching spirit-like out over precipice, then attacked a gully cleaving a rock fortification and faced bizarrely strewn boulders that formed chimneys and chutes.

The sky loomed nearer, and the world began to recede on all fronts—desolate plains an unfurled banner toward the falling sun, mounts Livermore and Locke bastions to the north, a thousand feet of open space infinity at our feet—leaving in its wake only solitude, utter tranquility. And just three hours from the moment we had looked up to study the summit from a third of a mile below, we stood taller than a mountain thirty-six million years in the making.

And we were satisfied.

PART 3

The Past

A meat-eating dinosaur's track southwest of Girvin.

The Girvin Site Dinosaur Tracks

𝑇hey remain as mute testimony that long ago the Pecos country held an order of life that is no more.

Embedded in the limestone of a creek bed southwest of Girvin, where mesas rise from the creosote lowlands of the Pecos River, the well-defined impressions indicate West Texas once was vastly different than today. Slashed by reefs and spanned by flats that flooded with the tide, it was a terrain roamed by creatures seen today only in fanciful imagery. It was an environment that since has been subjected to rebirth, a lost world now as long-dead as the great lizards that waded its shallows.

In 1965 a Texas Highway Department field party came this way to repair a highway, cutting a swath between low hills where tidal flats once had reflected sky. Some say a Southern Union employee already had beheld the mysteries of these knolls. At any rate, during lunch break the laborers wandered up the bed of a dry wash—and the tracks reached across the ages and caught them by the collars.

They were three-toed, twenty-one inches long, seventeen inches wide. A pace of five feet nine inches was apparent. Nearby were smaller tracks, linear markings, crisscrossed trails. It was an embodiment of the past, staring them in the face.

Dr. Wann Langston, professor of geology at The University of Texas and later director of the institution's Vertebrate Paleontology Laboratory, was summoned. The similarity to the foot structure of certain fossilized bones found elsewhere first led him to believe they were *Camptosaurus* tracks, then later, a related group of plant-eating dinosaurs known as Iguanodons. Then in the late 1980s, UT graduate student in geology Jeff Pittman—described by Langston as knowing "more about dinosaur tracks in Texas than anybody alive"—determined they were made by a group of moderate-to-large carnivorous dinosaurs ninety-five to one hundred million years ago.

"There are two or three track ways of different animals in that small drainage," said Pittman. "If you look at the prints upstream, they start to fall into a typical meat-eater track, which [has a] narrower toe print and ends in claw marks. The meat-eater that we have skeletons from in the region [north-central Texas and south-central Oklahoma] is called *Acrocanthosaurus*. It was a *big* meat-eater, rivaling *Tyrannosaurus rex*. We can never say that *this* particular animal left *this* particular track; we can only say that of the possibilities, this is the best candidate."

A close relative of the better-known carnivore *Allosaurus*, *Acrocanthosaurus* stretched twenty-six to forty-two feet from tail to snout, stood six and a half feet high at the hip socket (with the head angling forward to rise another several feet), and weighed up to 3.18 tons. A skull two and a half feet long bore powerful jaws and serrated teeth and, at the nasals, sharp ridges of horn that— given the leverage of a flexible and mighty S-curved neck—could have delivered dire head blows. Strong forelimbs a yard long held three fierce claws for seizing prey and tearing carcasses. The creature moved along agilely on moderately long hind limbs, extending its lengthy tail out behind for balance.

"The principle difference between *Allosaurus* and *Acrocantho-saurus*," noted Pittman, "is the enlarged neural spine—a fin that went down the backbone, which is where *Acrocanthosaurus* gets its name: *acro* meaning high, *canth* meaning spine."

This distinguishing "sail" ranged in height from almost a foot along the neck and tail to perhaps eighteen inches on the back. While the fin may have served as an identifying characteristic to rivals or mates, it also may have provided expanded muscle support for the back. Too, the spines may have performed as solar panels or heat radiators, allowing the reptile to regulate its body temperature simply by turning broadside to the sun or facing it.

Acrocanthosaurus may have been relatively long-lived, judging from track and fossil records. "We have small tracks and large tracks," noted Pittman. "Also, with fossils, we find young ones and old ones, [and] pretty commonly we find evidence of bone breaking and then rehealing, quite commonly the ribs or foot bones. So some of these animals probably had pretty rough lives. They sustained injuries and lived past them. So maybe from that information you can [infer] that some of them lived for many years."

Acrocanthosaurus may have hunted in packs, preying on ten-to-fifty-ton Brontosaurs or on Iguanodons—three-to-five-ton plant-eaters ten feet high and twenty-five feet long—in the shallows of a then-watery Texas. "The Llano area was sort of a central island," said Langston, "and sometimes this island was connected with the mainland to the north and sometimes separated. That whole part of the world was similar to the coast of Ethiopia and the Arab lands today, with the climate hot and the island's interior dry and desert-like."

It was the plain separating true ocean from true land that gave birth to the tracks in the Pecos country.

"Many of these track-bearing layers, sediments, that we see like there at the Girvin site were laid down on tidal flats," said Pittman.

[The] shoreline then of the ancestral Gulf of Mexico came across West Texas, around the Llano uplift and up northward into southern Oklahoma. And all along the shoreline there were really broad tidal flats, like you might see today in the Persian Gulf or places in Australia. And the dinosaurs [were] walking across them. It's difficult to say what they were doing. We have the tracks of plant-eaters like *Iguanodon* on the same layers with meat-eating dinosaur tracks. So it's

The Girvin Site Dinosaur Tracks

easy to get the meat-eaters out there because there were obviously plant-eaters out there. [But] you have a little harder time explaining why the plant-eaters are out there in the first place. It might have been hot and they might've just been going to the water to wade around.

Amplified Langston: "It has been suggested that these Iguanodons may have spent their lives moving in herds—some of them very large—from one little island to the next. The islands supported groves of mangroves and other plants."

As *Acrocanthosaurus* stalked the plant-eaters across those flooding tidal lands, footprints became impressed in the stiff mud. "Sedimentation . . . was very slow, so they filled up gradually with overlying muds and limes and were preserved in that way," explained Langston.

Through almost one hundred million years they were preserved—and then came man in the 1980s, discoloring the rock with plaster of paris casts, chipping away, vandalizing and removing tracks that already were ancient even when the Davis Mountains just beyond the horizon exploded to life. Still, at least a dozen tracks [along with linear erosion marks] remain clearly visible just one hundred yards off U.S. 67-385, with indications that many more must exist beneath overlying rock shelves.

Although the tracks are only one of about fifty known sets throughout the state, they are significant from a geographical standpoint.

"These are the farthest west tracks that I've seen in Texas," noted Langston.

"They're way out away from the other track sites that are known," added Pittman. "The closest one would be [on] the Middle Concho River [in] Irion County. The next closest would be west of San Antonio [in] Kinney and Medina counties." Westward, meanwhile, no other tracks are known to exist short of central New Mexico.

The Pecos country tracks, as well as the others, loom as windows into the distant past. Yet for every shred of evidence they grant, questions surface. Why did these nonpareil lizards fail to survive? A slow, steady change in environment? Sudden cataclysm? A comet?

Toss the questions to the wind in this land of mesa and creosote and the only answers are the hollow echoes of your own cries.

Midland Man

❧

*W*here skyscrapers now rise in the land of the Pecos, nomadic peoples once trod through grasslands and alpine forests in search of game. It was the late-Pleistocene, 9,000 years B.C., and the ancestors of the American Indian long-ago had crossed the land bridge at the Bering Strait in a southward migration to the tip of South America. In the Pecos country, some settled to pursue the great wooly mammoth, behemoths of tusk and sinew. Or, perhaps, it was the prehistoric antelope, camel, or horse roaming the uncharted vastness that streaked their lances with blood.

The hunters. The hunted. Sometimes, they were the same, made so by the threatening fangs of a prehistoric wolf.

In a lake bed along Monahans Draw six miles southwest of present-day Midland, one such Indian succumbed—whether to disease or beast, no one ever would know. There, for centuries that became millennia, the remains lay fossilizing, slowly being buried beneath ever-shifting dunes of sand.

The winds blew; the dunes migrated. In June 1953, Keith Glasscock of Pampa, a pipeline welder and amateur archaeologist, was scouring blowouts—bowled areas created by wind action within sand dunes—on land owned by Clarence Scharbauer when the find of a lifetime turned up at his feet.

Human skeletal remains.

Sensing they might be of great antiquity, Glasscock carefully gathered only the surface fragments in danger of being lost to the wind—a portion of a skull, a rib, and two metacarpals (bones of the hand)—and mailed samples to Fred Wendorf at the Laboratory of Anthropology in Santa Fe, New Mexico.

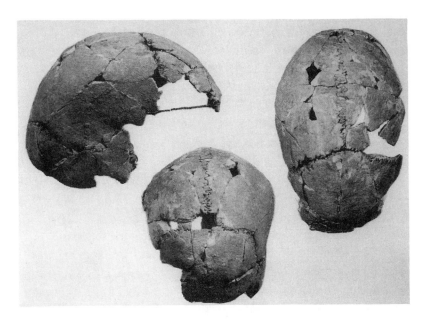

Three views of the Midland Man skull. (From The Midland Man Discovery *by Fred Wendorf, Alex Krieger, and Claude Albritton, The University of Texas Press, 1955)*

"He not only recognized a human skeleton, a skull," said Dr. Wendorf, "but he refrained from digging and tearing up. Here's an example of a wonderful relationship between amateur and professional in advancing our knowledge."

The samples excited Wendorf, and on October 29, 1953, the two men and several other archaeologists conducted a dig at the site, where sand dunes one mile long, one-half mile wide, and forty feet high lay adjacent to Monahans Draw. They uncovered three additional skull fragments, another rib section, and another metacarpal, as well as scores of bone flakes which were not identifiable as human. Additional excavations in February 1954 and in 1955 added supporting evidence: Paleo-Indian stone projectile points, grinding tools, scrapers, twenty thousand flint chips, blackened caliche from primeval hearths, and bones of the horse, bison, mammoth, sloth, and four-horned antelope.

"The antelopes gathered around the waterhole; man was there to hunt them," said Dr. Alex D. Krieger, one of the original investigating archaeologists.

Careful analysis of the narrow skull, which resembled that of a modern-day Indian, indicated Midland Man was not a man after all, but a woman who died at approximately age thirty.

Subsequent scientific dating suggested that she had died ten to eleven thousand years ago, and Glasscock's find suddenly assumed vast importance: He had uncovered the oldest substantial human skeletal remains ever found in the Western Hemisphere.

"It is unique," Wendorf reflected decades later from his office at the Department of Anthropology at Southern Methodist University. "I don't know of any other . . . fossil finds of human remains in the Western Hemisphere . . . [that are] older. There's been scraps of bones found that are that age or maybe a little bit older, but they have just been scraps. They were cremated burials up in the Dakotas."

Wendorf said that while the skeleton has proven difficult to date directly, scientists deduced its age through geology, archaeology, and chemical analysis. "These Midland artifacts found with the skeleton have been dated, at other places, around 10,800 years ago. This is the major indication of age, plus the chemical analysis of the skeleton."

After the original excavation, Wendorf and Dr. Ulf Hafsten of Norway undertook considerable study to determine the environment in which Midland Man lived. Fossil pollen recovered from Juan Cordona Lake basin in Crane County, Black Water Draw between Clovis and Portales, New Mexico, and another lake bed near Lubbock indicated that millenia ago the area "was a very different environment than today, a very different landscape," said Wendorf. "At that time the High Plains may have been open woodland with pine, spruce, and some piñon along the stream courses with grasses on the uplands."

Even four decades after the Midland find, Southwestern archaeologists and anthropologists still considered it a milestone in the study of man in the Western Hemisphere.

"I feel that the remains are a very significant find," said Wendorf. "It was the first generally accepted human skeleton from the New World that was of late-Pleistocene age. It gave us our first view of what the earliest Americans looked like."

"Among the group of human remains in the New World, it's among the very important specimens," said Dr. Christy Turner, physical anthropologist at Arizona State University. "Any find in that probable time range is important and, of course, the more material we have, the more reliable become our statistical instances of who these people were, where they were coming from, and what they were doing."

Midland Man, said Turner, obviously was a relatively close descendant of prehistoric Indians who crossed into North America by a land bridge in the Bering Strait.

Midland Man is close to having good association [with those first Indians], but it's not the good firm association we'd like. What I'm waiting for is a human under a mammoth with Clovis points in the mammoth. Some people feel that humans got here before 15,000 years ago. Another school says the hard evidence of the initial occupation of the New World is somewhere around 12,000 to 13,000 years ago. I tend to fall into the camp that looks into the hard evidence. I would simply have to say that there is not much strong evidence for anyone being here much before 12,000 years ago.

The Pecos country's claim to the most ancient human remains found in the New World has not been without argument.

"There have been a whole series of dates [assigned the skeleton] over the years—some based on experimental techniques—and what you end up with is a dozen different dates and take your pick," said Dr. David Meltzer, Wendorf's colleague in the Anthropology Department at SMU.

"One of the problems in assessing the age of the Midland Man find is that it was a surface find," said Dr. Dee Ann Story, director of Texas Archaeological Research Laboratory in Austin.

The early 1990s found Meltzer trying to determine Midland Man's age by dating the sediments in which it was found—a "back door" approach made necessary by the advanced mineralization of the skeleton.

"There are techniques," explained Wendorf, "[in] which you can extract amino acids from old bones and then direct date the amino acids. But [in] the skull, the protein and collagen in the bone has been so mineralized that it doesn't give enough amino acids to be direct-dated. That [mineralization] in itself is not an indication of great age; it could happen in six to seven thousand years."

Meltzer noted that even if Midland Man is only 7,000 years old, it still would represent a rare skeletal find from that time, as well as document human bone attrition during the Altithermal—a 2,500-year warm age which savaged West Texas beginning about 5,000 B.C. "What struck me as interesting," he said, "is that the teeth [all from the upper jaw] are heavily, heavily ground. . . . That would fit in nicely with an Altithermal burial. The Altithermal is a type of drought; there's lots of dust blowing in the air; there's lots of grit. And when you're eating vegetable material and plant parts with a lot of grit on it, you have excessive teeth wear." He added that bison teeth dating to the Altithermal Age display unusually high dental wear from chewing plant matter covered with "sand and grit."

Despite attempts to assess its age directly, Midland Man thus far has not fallen prey to high-tech dating methods that have reduced other North American skeletal finds to "also-rans."

"There have been several new techniques applied to other skeletal remains that had been considered to be about the same age or older," said Dr. Christopher Hill, an archaeologist at Southern

Methodist University. "And almost all these others have turned out to be [only] several thousand years old instead of over six or eight thousand years old."

Too, the original 1950s study of Midland Man reigns as a highly regarded prototype.

"It's really quite a pioneering effort that still holds up in terms of the scientific results," said Hill. "If you look in the classic texts on North American archaeology, this study is considered one of the first applications of the use of interdisciplinary work, that is, cooperation between geologists and archaeologists. It initiated a series of studies that have continued since that time, cooperation between geologists and archaeologists and other natural scientists trying to study that part of Texas and then to put that in the larger framework of North American pre-history."

Midland Man—or Woman—lies peacefully preserved at Southern Methodist University now, far removed from prehistoric West Texas where she once walked. Though ten or eleven millennia have passed, she stands taller than ever, with a foresight that is astounding. It was not until the advent of ranching and oil enterprises that modern-day people swarmed into the Permian Basin, but she had been aware of this land's attributes long before. The so-called "pioneers" of the nineteenth and twentieth centuries merely trod in her ancient footsteps.

Mustang Springs

☙❧

*A*pproach Mustang Draw where its arid narrows sink into wind-sculpted fields of south Martin County and imagine.

If darkness veils the sky, forget the glow of Midland-Odessa in the west; if daytime rules, wipe clean the image of nearby pavement and homes dotting the bordering bluffs.

And go back.

A century. A hundred centuries. Back to the 1800s when emigrant wagons creaked up the banks under the heavy loads of kegs just-filled from a spring pool, and back into time immemorial, when Indians with forgotten names lived forgotten lives beside its bubbling waters.

Mustang Springs, as it became known, has been dry for half a century now, ever since farmers began irrigating nearby in the 1940s. But that same hand of man that now rings its death knell once turned stick and ground-stone tool to its dry bed in order to effect a rebirth of its life-giving waters.

It was 4600 B.C., and a warm age gripped the Pecos frontier and would not relinquish it for millennia. For four thousand years already, Indians had journeyed to the springs to camp on its sentineling bluffs, gather food, and hunt the animals attracted to its shores. The ponds always had quenched their thirst, for here the underground formations held cracks that allowed aquifer waters to rise and fill a natural basin in the bedrock. Then, almost imperceptibly at first, the waters began to turn alkaline and the ponds to grow smaller, until finally ripples only of dust went crawling across their beds before the whipping wind.

And these forgotten Indians turned to digging wells— thousands of them, likely, during the next two hundred or more years.

"It had long been supposed that during the Altithermal [warm age], people just left the High Plains, because of the drought, the severity of the climates," said Southern Methodist University archaeologist David Meltzer, who uncovered more than sixty wells in a one hundred twenty-square-yard area at Mustang Springs in 1987. "What we've discovered here is that, in fact, people stuck around. The reason that we don't see much Altithermal evidence [of human occupation in West Texas] is that it's deeply buried down in these draws."

The Mustang Springs wells, though long-filled by 1987, yielded their secrets because Meltzer and his assistants recognized the sedimentary difference between the fill material and the nearly vertical walls. Upon excavation, they found that most were circular, oval, or double-lobed and of similar diameter, a mean of twenty-eight inches. Only in their depths (four inches to five and one-half feet) did they differ significantly, indicating that water—purified by the filtering properties of the surrounding soil—could be reached at levels that varied with the respective dates of digging.

"What that's telling us is that these groups are cycling through the area; they're not staying for particularly long periods of time," explained Meltzer.

They're just coming in, they're watering, they're maybe doing a little hunting, gathering, in the area, and then they're moving on. The reason is that [if] you stick in an area like this for a little while, pretty soon you're going to hunt out the local animals and gather up all the plants there are to gather. So they were probably coming through here annually or seasonally.

Basically, the wells were dug 6,800 to 6,600 years ago [determined by radiocarbon dating]. We may well find earlier or later ones were we to excavate more of this site. Or it may be that these groups, after around 6600 [before the present], decided that life was too hard, and left.

Archaeologist David Meltzer at the site of the excavation that revealed dozens of prehistoric wells.

Although Meltzer and his associates failed to discover animal bones or other food sources associated with the wells, they did document the presence of American buffalo, or bison, at Mustang Springs two thousand years prior to that time.

"There's a layer of dead bisons out there," noted Meltzer. "They date back to about 8780 [before the present]. Whether that represents a human bison kill, or whether that just represents three or four bison who just happened to die on the edge of an old pond, is hard to say."

Modern climatic conditions assumed control of Mustang Springs's fate approximately three thousand years ago, said Meltzer, bringing life-giving waters to its ponds again. The pools likely reigned uninterrupted on into historic times that saw (in the late 1700s) Comanches from the headwaters of the Arkansas and Red rivers ride the War Trail southward a thousand miles into Durango, Mexico. And millennia after those forgotten well-diggers had sought only life at its dusty surface, Mustang Springs yielded its waters to fierce warriors bound for bloodshed in Mexico.

No one knows when the first white man drank from its pools, but visitant Randolph B. Marcy gave the site its present name. Escorting a party of westward-bound emigrants as far as Santa Fe, New Mexico, in 1849, Marcy—a U.S. Army captain charged with determining a practical east-west route—bore to the south in heading for Fort Smith, Arkansas. His course carried him beneath the towering wall of the Guadalupe Mountains, through the white sand hills of the present counties of Ward and Winkler, and on toward the rising sun.

September 29, 1849, found Marcy following the horse paths of the War Trail, but the Indian threat was not as immediate as that of this arid land—a "high plain of the Llano Estacado." Fearing they might have to endure sixty-five miles of virtual desert before gaining the next water hole, Marcy and his party nevertheless discovered water only sixteen miles from the previous camp.

After a two-night rest, men and animals pushed onward October 1 and, on the southern edge of present-day Martin County, spilled down into the narrow valley of Mustang Draw and "discovered" an important water source. It was "a small lake . . . where it is thought there will be water at all seasons," recorded Marcy. "It is about three feet deep, covers several acres of ground, and has rushes growing in it."

Marcy noted the numerous wild mustang trails leading to and from the lake, and memorialized those animals which had been introduced into North America by Spanish *conquistadores*. "This lake I have called Mustang Pond. As the horse requires water every day, he would not probably stay at a place where it could not be found at all times."

Lieutenant Nathaniel H. Michler, tracing Marcy's route in the opposite direction three months later, also made note of Mustang Springs.

"There was nothing to indicate their presence," he recorded. "A few scattering chaparral bushes were growing within half a mile of them, but in proximity to the water were no trees or bushes of any kind. A low prairie of about a hundred acres in extent, in form very nearly circular, and bounded by low bluffs, composed principally of white limestone, contains several small ponds of water— one or two pretty deep, and the rest not containing much water."

Noting the several springs that bubbled up in the ponds, Michler sampled the water and found it "flat and sweet, being slightly brackish." He judged the pools to be permanent, not only from the approaching animal trails and the mustangs he saw watering, but from the "quantity of flag and other vegetable matter growing in and about them."

Paving the way in 1854 for the eventual laying of the Texas and Pacific Railroad, Brevet Captain John Pope and his contingent suffered the pangs of thirst as they crossed the area from west to east.

John Pope (National Archives)

"From various accounts, we anticipated meeting with water to-day in more than one pool on our route," Pope wrote on March 28, 1854. "Parties were sent out in every direction to look for it, and our anxiety was increased as each of them returned with an unsuccessful report. The animals were now showing symptoms of wanting it."

Mustang Springs

Their only hope was to forge onward toward Mustang Springs.

"We halted once during the day to rest our animals," Pope continued, "and then proceeded at a steady pace. The grass was good until within six miles of our camping-place, when it changed, becoming poor and full of weeds."

Forced to make a dry camp again that evening, Pope found insufficient water in their kegs even for cooking, "through the injudicious conduct of some of the command in drinking it during the day." He proceeded to punish the offenders, but he could do nothing about the wolves which drove away their flock of thirty-two sheep that night.

Early the next morning Pope and his men moved on across the rolling prairie and reached Mustang Springs at 10:30 a.m. They found that the springs comprised "several lakes or large pools, which are highly saline. . . . These lakes are about three miles in length, and run north 20 degrees west, and south 20 degrees east. They are enclosed by gentle eminences, on which the grass is better than in the bottom."

Camping before the easternmost pool, Pope found it less salty than the others. "It is slightly sulphurous, but not very unpalatable. There are some holes dug around, in which the water is somewhat better than in the bottom."

Wolves had greeted the party the night before; now it was time to be perused by the real rulers of the land—Indians.

"We met a party of Kiowas, who had a large number of horses and ponies, and were returning with them to their own country from Mexico," wrote Pope. "It is needless to say these animals had been stolen. The chief met us near our halting-place, and showed a friendly spirit."

Conditions were not always as affable between the U.S. Army and the tribes which rode the War Trail. In the last days of that dreaded path, in fact, Comanches avoided Mustang Springs and dug their own wells away from the immediate area.

"They were digging them not because this was a drought episode; they were digging them for defensive and strategic purposes," explained Meltzer, who authored a paper on the subject. "They were being dug in the 1870s, and the 1870s was a fairly wet decade, not a dry decade. But they didn't want to go to the ponds and the springs because that's where the U.S. Army was hanging around. So they dug wells somewhere in these draws, knowing they'd get water."

Assessing the Indian threat to West Texas in an 1875 campaign, Lieutenant Colonel William Shafter found ample water, mesquite-root fuel, and grass at both Mustang Springs and a site six and a half miles to the west.

"The water at both these places is in great abundance," he wrote, "hundreds of buffalo watering at them daily, not exhausting them."

For millennia Mustang Springs had given life; now it was time to harbor death. For the last significant buffalo slaughter in the region clouded its ponds with rifle smoke, as Joe S. McCombs and other hunters sent the reports of their large-caliber Sharps weapons echoing between the guarding bluffs in late 1878 and early 1879.

"Although I stayed out from September until the middle of March," recorded McCombs, "my entire kill was 800 hides. Buffalo were scarce and wild and started north on their very last migration before their usual time. But they never got back to their summer ranges. . . . I do not recollect having seen a buffalo on the range after my return from my last hunt."

More than a century later, evidence of that carnage may have surfaced at Mustang Springs.

"We found a bison bed which may be historic in age," said archaeologist Meltzer of his late-1980s field work at the site. "It said in the historic accounts that the last big buffalo kill in this area took place at Mustang Springs in 1879. The traces of it might actually be out there."

Today, Mustang Springs and its dry lake lie peacefully hidden to all but a few old-timers who remember fishing and swimming in its waters. Except for the rare rains which give it the illusion of permanence, only the sea-like odor of its briny bed testifies to its once-flooded confines.

Like those long-forgotten well diggers and an entire generation of nineteenth century wagoners and military men, it is now but a phantom.

Camels, Ships of the Trans-Pecos

They made port on the Texas Gulf Coast, carried awesome loads across the trackless wastes of the Big Bend, helped expand the American frontier.

Camels.

Ships of the desert.

Bizarre beasts which could travel through desolation for weeks without watering and, even when rocks slashed their feet, survive while the hardiest of mules succumbed. Their ability to squeeze nourishment from scant desert herbage—even thrive on it—amazed critics, and they adapted just as easily to mountain crags where snow climbed to the joints of their legs.

These were the camels of the United States Camel Corps, and the Pecos frontier recorded their footprints during much of this unique experiment conducted just prior to the Civil War.

The first suggestion that camels be employed for military purposes in the Southwest came in 1836, when Major George H. Crossman proposed the idea to Major Henry C. Wayne. It was Wayne who became obsessed with the notion, and when Jefferson Davis became secretary of war in 1853, Wayne convinced him to undertake the experiment.

Congress, acting on Davis's request, appropriated thirty thousand dollars in granting approval March 3, 1855, "for importation of camels and dromedaries [one-humped camels] to be used for military purposes."

And the camel era of the Old West had begun, with seventy-seven of the beasts to roam the frontier during the next few years.

A precedent for the military use of camels had been set thousands of years before by Asiatics and later Romans, and even as the United States implemented its plan, the French Saharan Camel Corps campaigned in Algeria. Officers had discovered that camels loaded with six hundred pounds could travel twenty-five to thirty miles a day through rugged terrain, while those bearing dragoons could trek seventy miles in only twelve hours.

Still, U.S. officials approached the initiation of its own camel corps with some trepidation and solicited Greeks and Turks as handlers. One such herdsman, Hadji Ali—better known as "Hi Jolly"—gained lasting fame, and his Arizona tomb is marked today by a statue of a camel.

After a long journey by ship from Egypt and other Mideast locales, the first thirty-four camels bearing the brand of the U.S. Army went into a frenzy on May 14, 1856, when they stepped onto Texas soil at Indianola, 120 miles south of Galveston. "[They] became excited to an almost uncontrollable degree," according to Wayne's log, "rearing, kicking, crying out, breaking halters, tearing up pickets, and by other fantastic tricks demonstrating their enjoyment of the liberty of the soil."

A U.S. Army camel secured for a gale aboard ship. (Barker Texas History Center, The University of Texas at Austin)

Camp Verde, near modern-day Kerrville, became head-quarters for the camel brigade, and in the expeditions launched from that Hill Country outpost into the brutal desert of the Trans-Pecos, the animals soon proved their worthiness.

Physiologically, the camel seemed designed for such an environment. While many mammals gathered food with their tongues and sustained loss of vital fluids in the process, a camel accomplished the task solely with its unusually mobile lips. It could subsist on thorny bushes, scrub desert flora, and foul-tasting weeds avoided by other mammals. Its thirty-four teeth—particularly the razor-sharp front ones—allowed it to pierce pulpy plants horses and mules could not.

The camel's hump, once thought to be a reservoir for water, actually consisted entirely of fatty tissue which it converted into moisture and energy during the rigors of a savage journey. Because of this unique metabolic process, it could lose up to one-fourth its body weight without suffering a loss of strength.

While a camel normally gulped twenty to thirty gallons of water every three days, it was so efficient at extracting moisture from shrubbery, it could survive ten months without actually drinking. Even in the most arid environment where herbage was scarce, it could carry heavy loads over great distances for as long as ten days without watering.

The blowing desert sands were of little consequence to a camel, with its double eyelashes and ability to close its ears and nostrils tightly. Its sure-footedness in all terrain except streams was legendary: The position of its eyes in its head was such that it normally looked at the spot where the front legs were to be placed next, and the feet, upon meeting the ground, spread to give the beast a broader base of support than any comparably sized mammal.

And those dimensions were considerable, a factor equalled by its longevity. Standing seven feet at the shoulder and weighing generally more than one thousand pounds, it had a life expectancy which approximated that of many of its frontier masters—forty years.

These were the qualities of the animal that Jefferson Davis described as possessing "endurance, docility, and sagacity."

The personality of camels, however, was a matter of some debate. The animals fought frequently and unnerved horses with their strong odor. The temperament of the males was especially unpredictable, as one private at Camp Verde discovered when he decided to cure his steed of its stubbornness with a swift kick to the belly. The animal turned and spat a reeking cud in his face and, when the man attacked with a club, ripped his arm open to the bone with its teeth.

This proclivity of the males toward moodiness resulted in the predominant use of females in the Big Bend expedition conducted in 1860 by William H. Echols, brevet second lieutenant and topographical engineer. Charged with exploring the backcountry of the Trans-Pecos and selecting a site on the Rio Grande for a possible military post, Echols's contingent consisted of thirty-one infantrymen, fifteen pack mules, and twenty camels and their attendants.

The brigade, with a capacity for carrying five hundred gallons of water, left San Antonio June 11, 1860, bound for Fort Davis, then an isolated mountain outpost. The first real problems developed June 30 after it crossed the Pecos River, which would be the last surface water for many days in the sun-broiled wasteland. While ascending a mesa, a pair of camels fell and burst two twenty-pound kegs of water. But the beasts' ability to carry heavy loads up steep bluffs with minimum difficulty nevertheless proved phenomenal.

"During the ascent," Echols recorded in his log, "they had to resort to their feat of walking on their knees, which they do when the inclination of the trail is very great and [they are] heavily laden, to throw the center of gravity equally over the fore legs, or on a slipping trail when their feet slip from under them."

The next day the terrain turned even more cruel: "rough, rocky, barren, dry, apparently no rain on the region . . . for a year," wrote Echols. "Every blade of grass dry and dead, and not of this year's growth. Our mules will not fare well—no forage and a very limited supply of water."

The camels, however, were a different story. "[They] have performed most admirably today. No such march as this could be made with any security without them."

But as the contingent marched deeper into arid wilderness, even the camels evidenced discomfort. "This is the fourth day since the camels drank, which was at the Pecos," Echols noted on July 2. "The camels display quite a thirst."

On July 3 the camels trudged onward with their heavy burdens. But the broiling rays of summer only worsened an already-unquenchable thirst. "The camels are continually bellowing, which I suppose, as it is unusual, [is] a sign of want of water," wrote Echols.

On that day, the mules became so weak the officers decided not to laden them, leaving the camels to bear extra packs over a thirty-mile course.

The lack of water soon became a matter of sheer desperation for the soldiers in Echols's charge. "Some of the men are very weak," he wrote, "and have several times reported about to give up and no water to drink. All we can tell them is, if they stop they must risk the consequences. . . . The men have a quart of water issued tonight, and have enough for two drinks tomorrow, but they are so feeble and thirsty that it all would not last them an hour if they could get to it."

To guard their canteens from one another, the men used them as pillows that night. The morning of July 4 saw hopes plummet further, recounted Echols, "as they proceeded to march with their two drinks of water, and not knowing when or where the next was to be had. . . . " Shortly afterward, however, Camel's Hump Mountain—which cradled the headwaters of San Francisco Creek—thrust into the sky fifteen miles distant, and the primal senses of the camels suddenly prevailed. "The animals exhibited a remarkable knowledge of approaching water sometime before reaching it, particularly the camels, which made a remarkable change in their speed ten miles from it," wrote Echols. "They had to be held back to keep them with the mules that before had been leading them."

By the time the party reached the first pools, the camels had endured five days without water in crossing one hundred twenty miles of some of the most desolate country known to man, where temperatures hovered above one hundred degrees in the shade. The mules, however, had watered twice and been relieved of their packs. In this first true test of the relative merits of the two herds, the camels had dominated. "[They] stood it well," said Echols, noting that even following two full days of rest, water, and forage, many of the mules were "worthless to us, with sore backs."

On July 10 the contingent stopped at Fort Davis to recuperate beneath the palisaded escarpment of the Davis Mountains. The camels remained strong, "doing finely, [with] no indications of having undergone any severities," wrote Echols. But even four days later, when Echols pointed the camel brigade to the southwest and gave the command to march, one soldier and nine mules suffering from physical deterioration stayed behind.

It was not until they reached Presidio del Norte on the Rio Grande and turned downstream to enter in earnest the badlands of the Big Bend that the camels developed noticeable infirmities— sore backs. Now, following only Indian trails or none at all, the expedition members were greeted with awe-inspiring vistas seen by few other white men. On July 25 Echols recorded their encounter with an astonishing natural wonder, Santa Elena Canyon: "Went to the river this morning . . . to see a wonderful curiosity which the guide told us of, a place where the stream runs through a mountain precipice, about 1,500 feet high. The opening is just the width of the stream, perhaps a little narrower than usual, the precipice springing vertically from the water to its summit."

On the next day the brigade located a likely spot for an outpost along a relatively pleasant wooded stretch of the Rio Grande. Upon turning back northward, however, the barrens of what is now Brewster County began to savage both man and animal.

"The camels were without water three days; the mules also, except a very limited supply last night," wrote Echols on July 30. "Both are beginning to show extreme exhaustion; the mules are lame and halt; the camels have several sore feet; their soles have actually been abraded off to the quick by the sharp cragged rocks, and others have sore backs—indeed, holes in the humps large enough to thrust in both fists. These sores do not injure them so much, being in the fleshy part of the hump, so long as they can be kept from the bone."

His first-hand experience in dealing with camels in the rugged Trans-Pecos led Echols to make suggestions regarding their care. "I would recommend to anyone using camels over rough country, in case of tender feet, to shoe them with a piece of [circular] hide, gathered around the leg by slipping cord; this will be found an absolute necessity in some instances."

By August 2 the demands of a wrenching expedition that had cost the use of many of the mules had begun to take its toll even on the camels. "Where we camped is about the point I wished to leave the trail last year for the Pecos, but the condition of the animals was too bad to undertake it, and our water too scarce," recorded Echols. "Now the condition of the animals is even worse, nearly every mule barefooted and lame, or exhausted, several of the camels almost unable to march at all from tender feet. We have water in our barrels, but to attempt the trip would be at the expense of several, both mules and camels. We will have to go to Fort Stockton to leave those that cannot go and have the mules shod."

On August 3, Echols noted that "several camels have sore backs but [are] fit for use" and "three have tender feet and march slowly; about two miles an hour on good roads. . . ." Another, he said, "has not browsed for two days; feet too tender to move about."

The expedition reached Comanche Springs and Fort Stockton August 4, and before embarking eastward Echols decided to leave behind a camel with an attendant, and two mules. By the time the contingent completed the return march to San Antonio, the superiority of camels over mules in the Southwest was well-established: Of fifteen pack mules, fourteen had died, been abandoned on the trail, or been left at army posts as useless, while nineteen of twenty camels had endured the ordeal.

Their value established in such torturous expeditions, camels seemed destined to play a major role in the development of the West. But with the outbreak of the Civil War the next year and the occupation of Texas by Confederate troops, the experiment was abandoned. By the time the nation reunited, the transcontinental railroad loomed on the horizon, and its completion in 1869 dealt a death blow to the camel corps.

But the impact of those U.S. Army camels on the American frontier was not over. While a few galloped over a civilian express route in Nevada in 1875 and others became midway attractions, many were turned loose or escaped into the desert. It was not unusual for many years thereafter for camels to be sighted in the wastelands, though the creatures left horses so distraught that both Indians and white men often sought to slay them on sight.

While camels never had lived apart from the care of man for thousands of years in their homeland, evidence began to surface in Arizona, California, and Texas that camels were not only surviving, but reproducing.

A boundary commission surveying the U.S.-Mexico border in 1901 witnessed camels "in their prime" in southern Arizona. In 1913 the crew of a Santa Fe Railroad train reported camels in the desert near Wickenburg, Arizona. In 1931 a man came upon a lone camel at a waterhole in southwest Arizona. In 1941 sightings of a camel were made along the eastern side of the Salton Sea in southeast California. In the 1970s, two men reported that while hiking Texas's Million Dollar Canyon in the Davis Mountains they sighted at a distance what seemed to be a deer; studying the animal through binoculars, they were astonished to learn it was a camel. Even today, according to some reports, old-timers in isolated portions of Arizona and California swear that hump-backed beasts still tread the desert floors.

Camp "Elizabeth"

𝓕oot-sore and beleaguered, the two buffalo hunters were nearing
so-called Camp Elizabeth along the North Concho River in the
1870s when they heard the war whoops of Comanches.

Already the hunters had walked more than thirty miles, and
for two days prior to the start of their desperate journey they had
been besieged by Comanches at the "big spring," site of Big Spring
in modern-day Howard County. Even now, several other members of their buffalo-hunting outfit were trapped at the oasis, and
their only hope lay in the two men and the "Camp Elizabeth" soldiers they hoped to summon.

The two men ran, stopping only to whirl and fire their powerful rifles at the marauders. They aimed for the horses, for they
knew that Comanches were but a slim threat when set afoot.

At the rocky point of a 100- to-150-foot cedary hill jutting
out over a grassy valley, the two hunters decided to make their
stand. In a natural depression between two uplifted rock slabs, one
man built a small fort of flagstone; the other fired, and fired again.
An Indian pony fell, then another. But still they came, human and
horse flesh enmeshed.

Three miles away at "Camp Elizabeth," just over a prominent
hill to the south-southeast, the sound of gunshots spurred troops
into action. Bugle blared; shod horses thundered; cavalrymen
charged. And the Comanches fled before the onslaught.

Battered and exhausted, the two men were carried to the
camp while a regiment of soldiers hastened to the big spring to
rescue their companions.

Though the oval defense rim of flagstone—some pieces abid-
ing two-to-three feet high—still crowns the point of a hill on what

The scattered foundation stones of Camp "Elizabeth." Inspecting the site is Delbert Dearen.

is now the VJ Ranch in Sterling County, the names of the hunters and soldiers long-since have faded into oblivion. The same fate almost has befallen the camp, the foundation stones of which lie piled and scattered midway between the North Concho River and a line of cedar-studded hills just off U.S. Highway 87 nine miles northwest of Sterling City. A Texas historical marker has pin-pointed the site since 1936, but even so, in labeling the ruins *Camp Elizabeth*, it muddles as much as commemorates.

"I can't find it referred to as Camp Elizabeth in *any* of our records," said John Neilson, historian at Fort Concho National Historic Landmark in San Angelo. "It was called Camp on the North Concho River."

The misnomer "Camp Elizabeth," in fact, may have stemmed from an impulsive joke instigated long ago by George McEntire, Sr., owner of the U Ranch which then comprised the camp.

"Actually, there's not a word of truth in the name on the marker," said his son George H. McEntire, Jr., born in 1908 and raised from infancy on the ranch.

Daddy and a friend of his were sitting in the den at the old George McEntire [U] Ranch, Sterling City, and the historical society called him and asked him, "What was the name of the old ruins across from the headquarters where the old fort used to be?" Daddy told him he didn't know, but a friend of his would probably know. He said, "I'll call you back."

So he asked this friend of his, "Do you have any idea what the name of the old ruins were across from the house?" His friend said, "No, but George, what was your grandmother's maiden name?"

Daddy said, "Frances Elizabeth Daniel."

His friend thought a minute—good, strong thinking—and he said, "Call 'em up and tell 'em that J. Frank Dobie said it was Camp Elizabeth."

In the folklore of "Camp Elizabeth," J. Evetts Haley sometimes assumes the role of that "friend," an allegation Haley denied. Regardless, said McEntire, both Dobie and Haley are men who, like his father, "always lived by the old axiom of *Never let the truth interfere with a good story.*"

Once maintained as an outpost by Fort Concho, situated fifty-five miles downstream, Camp on the North Concho may predate its parent military post. Here, as early as 1853 by one account, either Texas Rangers or soldiers set up stakes in defending the frontier against Indians. Officials chose the site with care; a few hundred yards distant lay the headwater springs of the North Concho River, the first perennially flowing waterway east of the Pecos.

Sterling County pioneer W. F. Kellis described the river as it looked in 1887: "It was then the most beautiful stream I ever saw. The water was as clear as crystal and ran the year round over its pebbly bed. Deep pools of clear, cold water existed where fish sported in great numbers. Beavers in large colonies built their lodges and dams from San Angelo to up the river to the head of the living water in the U [Ranch] pasture eleven miles up the stream from Sterling City."

From nearby bluffs, the Rangers or soldiers quarried stone for construction of a hospital, officers' quarters, sutler's store, kitchen, farrier shop, and stables and corrals.

"Some of the [buildings] were partially standing when I was a little fellow about three or four years old, along about 1912," said George H. McEntire, Jr. "You'll find the ruins of the officers' quarters over on the south side [of U.S. 87] and, evidently, the blacksmith shop, because there's been lots of old horseshoes and nails found in that area." Four "barracks-type" structures to the north of the present highway composed the major portion of the post, he added.

The officers' quarters reportedly measured twenty feet by thirty feet and the hospital twenty feet by fifty feet, though on-site study by members of Midland Archeological Society and Concho Valley Archeological Society in 1976 suggested otherwise for the latter building. They found foundations or mounds of four primary buildings on the north side of U.S. 87:

The southeasternmost ruins, situated about 124 yards north of the fence, measured fourteen feet by thirty feet, with a cut-stone opening indicating a door and center rock alignments hinting at two rooms. Nine yards to the north lay a rocky mound suggesting a second structure, eleven feet by eleven and one-half feet. Thirty-nine yards on to the west-northwest lay evidence of the largest building, twenty-seven feet by twenty-nine feet and possibly comprising four rooms. Another fourteen yards northward sprawled the best-preserved foundation, twelve feet by twelve and one-half feet. A small rock scatter north of the four buildings may have been a privy.

If Texas Rangers did predate the U.S. Army in encamping at the site, few stories of nearby skirmishes between Rangers and

A kettle unearthed at Camp Elizabeth.

Indians have survived. One extant account, however, involved a Ranger company commanded by Buck Barry.

While the main body of the company bivouacked at the headwater springs near Camp on the North Concho, Ranger M. N. Harrison strayed away to hunt. A buffalo dropped at the sharp report of his rifle, and as he knelt to skin the animal, gunshots suddenly peppered the ground at his side. He whirled about; a Comanche war party was upon him. Harrison fled on horseback across the plain, up a rocky hill, and down the far slope. His horse lost its footing and fell, throwing him. His leg shattered, Harrison was rescued by Rangers as they responded to the gunfire.

Upon the reoccupation of Texas by the U.S. Army after the Civil War, federal troops assumed many of the frontier duties of the Rangers. The Army established Fort Concho in 1867 at present-day San Angelo, and by the mid-1870s began dispatching troops to Camp on the North Concho. There, on the grassy plain sentineled by a fortification of gray hills, the buffalo soldiers tented and trained. These were Negroes, so-named buffalo soldiers by Indians who thought the soldiers' curly hair resembled the tufts of the buffalo. Fort Concho's primary interest in the site may have rested in the south-trending parade ground, where soldiers fostered riding techniques, and in the target range. The latter, situated near the base of the bluffs to the north, included target butts for both close- and long-range weaponry.

"There were a number of sub posts of Fort Concho that were set up, especially during the period of administration of Benjamin Grierson from 1875 to 1881," said Fort Concho historian John Neilson. "Every year [of the scout reports] you see companies going out to Camp on the North Concho, usually for target practice and other routine drills. I think you can probably infer that 'Camp on the North Concho' . . . at the head of the North Concho . . . is the same site as Camp Elizabeth. Usually they're not out there for more than a month or so at a time. So I think it was kind of like a temporary camp."

Neilson added that acting assistant surgeons or contract physicians generally accompanied troops into the field, though "most of the time serious [medical] cases were sent into Fort Concho. Now if somebody died out there, they may or may not have brought them all the way back in."

Such evidently was the case with two soldiers whose graves lie side-by-side on an elevated flat a few hundred yards north of the camp. W. F. Kellis recorded in 1943 that these were black enlisted men, one of whom died violently.

> The late Thomas Brennand Sr. told me that he was near the spot when one of these colored soldiers met his death at the hands of an enraged cowpuncher.. . . Camp Elizabeth was then a very lively place. Several hundred Negro troops were stationed there. At the time of the killing, a man with a barrel of fresh whiskey . . . was on the river at the spring that furnishes water for the camp, and was serving it out to everybody at so much per tin

cup. . . . The Negro was drunk and used abusive language toward the cowpuncher and he used a forty-five to put a period in the colored man's argument. . . . The cowboy who shot the Negro rode for tall timber where everything was clear and serene. . . . The other Negro soldier is said to have died a natural death.

Though a 1991 inspection of the graves, each capped with rocks laid out along an east-west axis, revealed no evidence of exhumation, Kellis further noted in 1943 that "I was also told that later the remains of these two Negro soldiers were moved and buried in a national cemetery."

By the 1870s, cattle kings began taking advantage of the stirrup-high grasses in the region. In 1876, D. A. Earnest and W. H. Holland established the U Ranch near Camp on the North Concho. Despite the occasional presence of troops at the camp and the confinement of Comanches to reservations, Indians remained a menace. In fact, the last documented raid by Comanches occurred in 1879 on the U Ranch within a rifle shot of Camp on the North Concho. From north of the Red River, Black Horse and twenty-five other Comanches fled the reservation to hunt buffalo, which by that time had been all but exterminated by white hunters. At the head of the North Concho, the Comanches butchered colts for food and stole several horses from the U Ranch, prompting a June thirtieth skirmish with cowboys and Texas Rangers a mile west of ranch headquarters. With Andy Jones and a man named Manning serving as scouts, the cowboys and Rangers—along with cavalrymen from Fort Concho—pursued the Indians to a fresh-water lake north of present-day Midland. There, on July 1, 1879, two Indians killed Ranger W. B. Anglin and several horses. Calling off the chase, Lieutenant C. R. Ward of Fort Concho ordered Anglin's body rolled in a saddle blanket and buried at the lake.

Until approximately 1886, the camp continued to foster weaponry and riding techniques and to safeguard emigrants, railroad surveyors, and the area's first settlers. But with the threat of

Apache depredations in the Southwest finally ending, the U.S. Army abandoned the post.

Absorbed into the rangeland of the U Ranch, the buildings became a hangout for drifters and desperados, a development which led ranch owners to destroy the roofs and give pioneer J. N. Kellis the rocks. Kellis hauled the stones to a site on the North Concho River eight miles northwest of Sterling City and constructed a dam, evidence of which remains.

But though the post was gone, there still abided nearby graves and empty holes which provided the stuff of legend.

"Down near the river there's a little ravine that comes in from across the highway," noted George H. McEntire, Jr., "and just on the east side of the ravine, where it goes into the Concho River, there's two graves. They're women folks who died on wagon trains going west. And the first one that died, they took the floor up out of the old kitchen in the foreman's house and built a casket for that body."

At the base of the hill immediately northwest of the post lies a depression marked by a clump of catclaw bushes. "When I was just a little fellow," said McEntire, "my daddy heard that something had been done over there, and they went over and found where there was a hole in the ground and the imprint of a box that had been removed. There was a rumor, or legend, that there were twenty-one jackloads of silver that had come through there and some of it had been buried in that area."

The presence of rock markers on the slope of the hill above stirred the imaginations of treasure seekers. "Years ago, there were two rows of rocks that went up the side of that mountain, very visible," McEntire noted. "And they went to two piles of rocks on top of that hill—that hill is the tallest one in that bunch of hills out there."

At the summit of that hill, a U Ranch employee once discovered one particular rock bearing apparent markings and removed it to ranch headquarters. Studying this "plat rock" in the late 1920s or early 1930s, an elderly treasure hunter from Loraine determined that it once had formed the point of two lines which, along with other clues detailed by the etchings, gave directions to buried bonanzas. Ralph Davis, then foreman of the U Ranch, accompanied the man on his ensuing search.

"He called me over there and said, 'Is there any such thing as two rows of rock?'" recounted Davis. "I said, 'Yeah, they're just about six feet apart and come right off that point over there.' You could see them three hundred yards before you got to them. That old man said, 'Let's go. So many steps from the end of those rocks there's going to be three big rocks in a triangle. Twenty-one feet from the last rock there's going to be another buried rock with an *X* cut on it.'"

Davis, however, was merely tolerant of the eccentric "old coot"—until he followed the man down the rock rows descending the slope.

"He stepped off down there and, sure enough, there those three old big rocks [three feet in diameter] were. One of them had been moved. He took a shovel and twenty-one feet from there he dug—and durned if he didn't dig that rock up with the *X* on it."

The find excited Davis, especially when the Loraine man told him the plat rock gave even more clues.

"He said, 'So many feet down this way from that [*X* rock] there's supposed to be a buried treasure, and so many feet that way from this is another bunch, and across the river is another.' He said, 'I'll go back home and come back Monday morning and we'll find them.'

"Well, a car ran over him and killed him Sunday morning when he was walking across the street in Loraine. And that was the end of that."

Several years later, however, Davis himself went looking after he had learned the art of dowsing.

"I could find those three rocks, but we took a backhoe machine out there and all we got was slivers [of the supposed treasure]. We dug up four or five of those thin slabs . . . and my brother took them to Big Spring to be analyzed, and they said it was silver."

131

Camp "Elizabeth"

George H. McEntire, Jr., however, believed the twin rows of rocks denoted not treasure, but an even more valuable commodity in the Pecos country.

"It's reasonable to assume," he said, "that those piles of rocks were put there to be able to see them for many miles to indicate water [at the North Concho springs], which was the most precious thing."

As the springs failed and the legends grew, the dust-laden wind slowly buried the foundations and artifacts of Camp Elizabeth, the apocryphal, and of Camp on the North Concho, the genuine. For the former, it meant perpetuity in the folklore of the people, but for the latter, it only showed how easily the years can garble history and truth.

PART 4

People

Derricks and Gushers

*H*e was the last of a breed, and like the old-time cowboy before him, he succumbed to the technology of a new order. But not before he wrote himself into the annals of West Texas as indelibly as the man who wore chaps and rode ramrod across the Pecos.

He was the cable tool driller, that salt-of-the-earth oil field legend who toiled day and night in the West Texas sands and mesa country in the hope of seeing black gold gush forth to blacken the sky.

Sometimes he succeeded. Often he didn't. But he persevered to the rhythmic nodding of the twenty-six-foot wooden beam of the rig, as, far below, a drill bit at the length of a manila rope or cable hammered into the earth's crust by power of gravity.

Drillers on rotary units, which spiraled into the ground by the whirring of drill pipe and bit, derided him as a "jarhead" because of the sledgehammer concept of cable tool drilling: lift the bit, let it drop, lift, drop, lift, drop, until six to ten feet has been accomplished; then bail it out and start again. And while the jarhead's rig steadily chiseled two-thirds of a mile through subterranean formations, he in turn slapped the moniker "swivelhead" on rotary operators. And all the while, this pioneer driller and his archetypal "tools" were spawning a forest of pumpjacks across land once shunned even by the coyote.

W. W. "Bill" Allman was one such man. In his sixty-two years in the oil fields—from 1915 to 1977—he drilled hundreds of oil wells and involved himself in legends of derricks and gushers.

"It was fun, it was daring, it was hard," he summarized.

Bill Allman holding a peavy, used in handling timbers on a cable tool rig.

Born in Arkansas City, Kansas, March 30, 1899, Allman began roughnecking in a refinery as a sixteen-year-old stripling, and by the time he was seventeen he had almost gotten killed in three separate accidents. He worked as a roustabout for a while in Dillsworth, Oklahoma, putting in four ten-hour days and two other full days walking a forty-mile stretch of pipeline to and from home in Arkansas City. But all the while, the romance of cable tool drilling summoned, and in 1917 he became an apprentice to an old-time driller. "You had to work at least a full well for nothing before anyone would hire you," he recalled. After his thirty-day "gratis" stint he hired on with a Star Machine cable tool outfit as a tool dresser. The driller's sole assistant, the tool dresser had among his duties the heating of dulled bits in a forge and reshaping of them by sledgehammer. In sand the bit would manage only a few feet before it needed "dressing"; in other formations such as salt or red rock it might drill five hundred to six hundred feet.

It was just Allman's luck to have a tough old driller for his first boss.

"He was a Swede, name of Johansson, big fellow," he remembered.

> He was the meanest old man you ever saw. And when he felt good, he kept you around that ol' hole listening to his rotten ol' dirty stories, and when he hurt, why, he done everything mean to you he could. He was so mean the contractor came out there one day and said, "Bill, if that driller does another thing to you or gets mean with you, just take this fork handle and knock his head off." A fork handle is about five times bigger than a bat. He wanted to let me know that he approved for me to hold up for myself. That made me feel good.

Five years of apprenticing and dressing tools culminated with Allman becoming a full-fledged cable tool driller in 1922. He drilled in the Kansas oil fields until lured to West Texas by the promise of ample work after Santa Rita Number One blew in near

Big Lake. Temporarily leaving his wife behind in Kansas, Allman came down in July 1928 to what he believed to be "a big lake of water."

Arriving first in San Angelo, he rode westward with another driller and a tool dresser and—in the wee hours of the morning—reached McCamey to sleep on the ground. Expecting to awaken to the lush greenery of a lake shore, Allman opened his eyes to desolate mesa country and a tent city.

"If I'd've had enough Kansas dollars I'da went home—I wouldn't have stayed a minute," he recalled.

McCamey, depraved by such notorious night spots as Trice Hotel, Bloody Bucket, and Green Parrot, was West Texas's own Sin City in those days. "Just say it, they did it," noted Allman.

He began working the oil fields, and before the year ended found himself in the newly established tent city of Crane, itself possessing red-light and gambling districts. Allman sent for his family, and for the next several years they lived in and out of Crane in a succession of tents and shotgun houses, most of which had no plumbing.

In those early days of Crane, he recalled, transients were too numerous to be counted. Most structures consisted of floors made of one-by-twelves and two-by-fours, with walls only three boards high and tents as roofs. Shotgun houses, meanwhile, were only one room wide and several rooms deep, with separate families living in each room and entrances only on the ends.

Men lived fast and died hard in the Depression oil fields of West Texas, but they had a code of honor about them which is unknown today.

"Nobody had a lock on anything—nobody *took* anything," remembered Allman, who noted that a man's handshake was better than a contract. "Honest, the drunkard then and the ol' boy that was a bum, he wasn't as dangerous as the same class of man today. He had an honor about him. You could pick those kinda guys up and they were grateful. They did like to fist-fight, but those ol' boys'd go to Fist City and whip the heck out of you and then get up and shake your hand and say, 'Well, I'll see you tomorrow,' and go on about their business."

Sometimes that proclivity toward "friendly persuasion" had humorous overtones.

"Gulf had a big ol' boy they called Ben Wray, and he was the nicest big ol' fellow you'd ever seen," said Allman.

> He was six feet fourteen—he didn't want to be called seven foot two. He sparred with Jack Dempsey. [In fact Dempsey—when challenged by Wray at the Manassa Mauler's Great Falls, Montana, training camp in 1923—shattered the larger man's jaw in less than thirty seconds.] One time ol' Ben Wray was driving along Crane's main block, and three men in another car didn't like the way he turned. So they drove up to him and the driver stuck his head out of the car and said, "Ol' buddy, if you'll park that thing I'll work you over." And ol' Ben said, "Well, I'll oblige ya." Ben just pulled around, parked, and sat there in his car and waited for those guys. They pulled up about middle of the street, bailed out of their car, and here they came. Ben saw they meant business so he just opened the door and began to unfold himself, and just before they got to him they began to stop. And there ol' Ben was, six feet fourteen, looking down on 'em, saying, "Well, still wanna take me on?"

The men opted for a fast getaway.

Although rotary rigs began making inroads in West Texas in the 1930s, the old "jarheads" yielded but grudgingly, and Allman purchased his own cable tool rig from his one-time boss Burt Weekly in 1946. Working twelve-hour "tours" (pronounced "towers") or shifts, seven days a week, usually fifty-two weeks a year, Allman and his employees hammered out a 3,200-foot well every four to five weeks. Today's modern rotary units can do the same in four to five *days*. Yet Allman always remained convinced the art of cable tool drilling should not have been allowed to die.

"Cable tool rigs drilled a straighter hole than rotaries ever thought of drilling," he said. "See, we drill ours up and down, and gravity makes you hang straight. A rotary goes around and around, and if they hit something hard on one side and it's soft on the other, the bit will go off. They'll get off eight to ten degrees—I never sold a well to anyone over five degrees, and I drilled a lot of 'em. And we could give 'em a well they could pump without wearing out rods and tubing and one that was a whole lot easier to produce."

Tales of tricks played upon oil field novices, or "weevils," and of brushes with catastrophe abound in oil patch folklore. A favorite stunt of veteran crews, recalled Allman, was to send a weevil to another rig to borrow a "skyhook"; that gang, in turn, would send him to a third, until the new hand had bounced around every rig in the area without turning up the requested tool. There was a reason for his failure—no such "skyhook" existed.

Veterans, too, proved the butt of pranks. On those rare occasions when a cable tool rig would shut down for a day, a driller might stuff overalls and a jacket with rags so that it resembled a man, tie it to the sand line, and hoist it to the top of the rig. When the relief hands came on at midnight and started the first bailing operation, they would be aghast at what appeared to be a man plummeting into their midst.

Dangers were ever at hand too, especially in the handling of nitroglycerin, which would be dropped into a well to break up subterranean formations. It was common for wells in the Crane area to flow sour oil and gas at regular intervals; during the lulls, nitro men would put in two or three runs of the explosive.

"Once you got it down in the hole quite a ways, it was all right—it'd probably go right straight on down," explained Allman. "But one time right out here [near Crane] this well went to flowing ahead of time. And this ol' boy had dropped one too many cases, and as he started putting more in the hole the well started bubbling over. It was gonna kill him anyway—he couldn't run from it—so he had to be cool. He was lucky he didn't get overcome with gas, but as they [the nitro charges] came out of the hole the ol' boy just got in there with 'em and hugged 'em and laid those babies down gently."

It wasn't until Allman's sixty-first year in the oil fields that poisonous gas finally got the best of him. "We'd already done the job on a well and were trying to get the tools down," he related. "It was making so much gas the driller had to turn his head to get fresh air. I finally got enough and walked away toward the doghouse and got out there and went down. If that's all it takes to die, it's very peaceable—you just fold up and go down and it doesn't hurt you. Soon as I got a little fresh air in my belly again I could get up."

But in 1977, after having drilled a well in his seventy-eighth year, Allman finally sat down for keeps in retirement. He was due a rest. Not only had he drilled hundreds of wells throughout Kansas and West Texas, but he also had devoted thirty-five years to public service as a school board trustee, hospital board member, city councilman, and mayor of Crane.

Energetic, ambitious, hard-working, persistent—they describe the cable tool driller, and Allman, who epitomized the craftsmen who plied their now-lost art.

Too, one final characteristic might be assessed this throwback to another era: sadness. "It's a shame, a crying shame, that they didn't go ahead and try to teach cable tool drilling in school and keep it in because there's lots of places now that could use 'em to good advantage, for less money, and do a whole lot better," Allman reflected quietly. "But it's too far gone now—I don't think they could ever revive it."

And so ends a legend.

Boxcars and Brakies

✠

*F*or four decades they have manned the trains that thunder across the Pecos country.

They are beset by wrinkles now, and a couple walk with kinks in their strides, beleaguered as they are by the aches and pains of more than half a century. But for Missouri Pacific engineer Bill Bain, conductor Linus Tucker, and brakemen Polly Adams and Moose Webb, the endless click of wheel against rail joints tolling off the miles has wrought a miracle, blending men's souls with the inanimate steel and wood of the railroad until today they are spiked together as closely as track and crosstie.

The open countryside slashed by Missouri Pacific right-of-way has harbored this unique bond for a combined total of almost a century and two-thirds, and may shape their futures as well. Other than for occasional backward glances around curves to check the mile-long series of boxcars, hoppers, and tankers, the eyes of the crew, like the glaring headlight of the locomotive, continually seek out the track which forever precedes them into the horizon.

There, where distance merges twin rails into one, a common destiny may await: a gasoline truck stalled on the track, a wrongly pulled line switch, a washed-out trestle, or an uprooted rail. Behind, they leave a trail of black smoke, a million-plus miles of track, and haunting memories.

For these railroaders are remnants of a past generation, stalwarts of the era of the steam locomotive which chugged and puffed its way into the legends of Texas. Throwbacks out of time, they have spanned the gap between the glamour of those lore-rich days and the fast-paced atmosphere spawned by the diesel engine.

Four in a row, these ultra-modern locomotives of Missouri Pacific Train 61 pummel into Big Spring switching yards from Fort Worth at daybreak as a thousand wheels clatter against rail. Behind, stretched out over a mile of track like a Texas rattler sunning, are the trailing cars: tankers poisoned by hydrofluoric acid and sodium hydroxide, piggybacks swaying under creosoted telephone poles, carriers gleaming with the chrome of new automobiles. Jerked throughout the night like the end of a popped whip, the caboose lunges in last, its red square forming a nub to the train like a partially formed rattle.

An ominous canyon steadily guts the freight yards from one end to the other as the train is switched onto a side track parallel to a hundred boxcars. It has been a long night, 258 miles of it since Cowtown, and the men who couple the cars and throttle the engines welcome the relative comforts of the red-brick depot.

The next crew—consisting of the four aging railroad warriors—gathers on the gravel before the main line as an eastbounder storms by, the gaps above the couplings revealing the locomotives of Train 61 like dancers in a strobe. The sun rising over a sea of boxcars casts engineer Bain's shadow to within inches of the flanged wheels running just inside the rail, ground as silvery as water tank icicles by years of steel meeting steel.

It's always been a matter of inches for Bain, who has experienced his share of jolts and lumps in train-car crashes and has narrowly escaped cataclysm equivalent to the explosion of a load of dynamite.

"When the gasoline trucks cross the tracks in front of you, you have some anxious moments," he reflects with brow furrowed like a weather-beaten crosstie.

Drivers don't realize, says the train crew, that a fully loaded one hundred-car freight speeding sixty miles per hour normally needs one and a quarter to one and a half miles to halt, and if the emergency brake is thrown—an act that always risks derailment— more than half a mile of track will still be plowed over before wheels cease to thunder.

143

Boxcars and Brakies

But that is something to mull over in the backs of their minds on down the line. For now, the eastbounder has stopped, and Bain and head brakeman Adams clamber across the coupling between a hopper and a tanker to become framed in the long corridor bordered on one side by Train 61 and forward Locomotive 3225.

Once inside, man becomes a part of machine. Fingers flip switches, find throttle, test a mile-long tunnel of air which brakes the cars. The control area is small, a brakeman's reach in length and the breadth of a boxcar. Ahead, eighteen-foot walls of freight cars loom on either side for half a mile, and peering at the tunnel of light at the end is like looking through the barrel of a shotgun, the locomotive a slug readied to be fired through. All the pre-run checks made, air brakes burst free with a great release of pressure and the engine lurches forward, straining under a load of 10.3 million pounds. Behind, eighty freight cars lengthen out, the couplings slamming taut in rapid succession. The locomotive reels down the track like a drunken pirate, the vibration of its wheels battering legs through metal floor. Diesel smoke belches skyward, singeing nostrils and drifting back over tanker, hopper, piggyback. The air horn, perched at the nose of the locomotive like an emblematic figure on a ship's prow, casts its shadow onto the sided cars, first crawling along their upper battlements, then sprinting with ever-increasing speed.

Train whistle blares, screams back from the bordering cars, and then the freight is in open countryside, headed for a sunset rendezvous with El Paso.

Situated in a small compartment at the right side of the cab, Bain takes his gloved hand from the throttle and eases back in his seat. He rests a scuffed cowboy boot against a wrench placed parallel to the floor for a foot support and squints at the terrain's brightness through his ebony-rimmed glasses. Against the indigo backdrop of flooded salt lakes through the window, his profile becomes a silhouette: cap bill crowning hair the color of an often-used rail, firm Roman nose, jowls creased by age.

But Bain's six-plus decades have not lessened his ability to control 5,088 feet of freight train powering its way across the Pecos country's rail network. If anything, the accumulated experience has added to his prowess, since the rails hold two-thirds of his years dating from the time he first climbed aboard an oil-burning steam locomotive as a fireman back in 1942.

While today the term "fireman" refers to an apprentice engineer, it lived up to its implications in those days, when he was responsible for keeping the fire blazing hot. World War II claimed Bain in 1944, but even then, the military recognized a life intrinsically identified with the rails and assigned him to the railroad battalion. He was released to pursue his railroad career out of a Big Spring base in 1946, and within a few months the controls of the locomotive were at his fingertips, never to leave them in the decades since.

The first big railroad curve out of Big Spring snakes under the train and couplings ease their grips, building up twenty feet of slack that will bang taut once the straightaway is reached. From the locomotive, Polly Adams looks back over the cars, checking for trouble. In a mile-long behemoth of wood and metal, occupied only at either extreme by crewmen, the curves allow the only opportunity to see the torso of the train. Once the freight reaches one hundred fifty cars in length—almost two miles—no curve is great enough to permit locomotive or caboose to be visible from the other, and crewmen are completely isolated but for radio.

The role of a brakeman, made legendary by the mournful railroad songs of Jimmie Rodgers in the 1920s and 1930s, is much the same today as it was a hundred years ago. Charged with making set-outs and pick-ups of freight cars along the line, the head and rear "brakies" have the most elemental contact of all with the train: throwing levers to couple and uncouple, attaching air brake hoses between cars or letting them explode free, directing the engineer with hand signals, clinging to a boxcar ladder as the wind becomes a sensual gale in their faces.

Adams, at a shade under six decades, is the youngest of the crewmen, having given but thirty-odd years to the weaving boxcars and clanging bells. To him, the routine of carrying a westbounder to Toyah and returning to Big Spring on the wheels of an eastbounder every day has submerged what glamour his job once might have held. "He was just makin' up songs," he says of Rodgers, the "Singing Brakeman" who yodeled the saga of the railroader into the annals of country music.

But he has learned he can't take his duties for granted—not when five thousand tons of train rise about him, with force great enough to pulverize a human body. "Dangers—you always have a few of 'em," he says, readjusting his bluejean-billed cap as the freight cruises down the tracks at fifty-two miles per hour, scaring up a pair of turkey vultures from the crossties. "When you have one, it kinda brings your attention to what you're doin'. If you don't watch, you can get a little lax. Anytime you work with heavy machinery, you don't have much leeway."

Rear brakeman Moose Webb, born in 1919, didn't have much leeway several years ago when he was on a fast freight crossing West Texas. Noticing something unusual from his position in the caboose, Webb began to check the cars ahead. On the tenth car forward from the caboose, he discovered a broken wheel—cracked three-quarters of the way around to a depth of half an inch. "I don't believe it would have gone much further without completely disintegrating," the trainmaster said later.

A broken wheel on a fast freight would have meant derailment—and had it derailed, says Webb, "it would've taken the caboose with it."

It was a life-threatening situation not unlike many others on the rails every week, but Webb's considerable experience—now forty years—held him in good stead, as it still does.

From Bain's position in the locomotive, downtown Stanton sweeps into view at forty miles per hour. Streets slash across tracks at regular intervals, and Bain's hand finds the air horn lever, the whistle shrieking all the way through town. Near the outskirts of the city, a truck crosses the track less than fifty yards from the barreling locomotive, and Bain takes a deep breath and just shakes his head.

But Adams is vocal. "If they get on there they're gonna get killed," he growls. "People've got the idea we can stop. We can put the emergency on, but we're still gonna hit 'em. Some ol' boy pullin' out in front of me, that don't bother me, if he wants to kill himself. It's when he's got a wife and whole buncha kids with him that bothers me."

Just the day before, the Fort Worth to El Paso train broadsided a pickup in downtown Midland, but that time the driver survived. Others have not been so lucky. A few years ago, recalls the train crew, several girls were killed in Odessa when their auto stalled on the rails. One of them managed to climb out in time, but froze on the tracks before the oncoming freight. Only her torso ever was found.

"You could take a flashlight and look on the front of that locomotive and see her face just as plain as anything," recalls Odessa trainmaster Ray Hanfeld, riding in Train 61's locomotive on this day. He grimaces. "Most times those things don't bother me, but that one did."

But motorists aren't the only ones endangered by the careless crossing of railroad tracks.

Adams nods at the bus-like door which opens to the Midland skyline ahead. "Near Monahans one year a train hit a truck, and a rock came through the forward engine door, slamming it back and cutting off a brakeman's leg," he says.

As the train stampedes nonstop through Midland at twenty-five miles per hour, Bain finally has his say about unwary drivers. "Boy, it's somethin' when you come by here on Saturday night and those bars right there," he says, sending the air horn blasting through the city. "They're just like a bunch of bees. They don't pay no more attention than anything."

Thirty minutes later the Loop 338 overpass hangs in the sky ahead on the outskirts of Odessa, and Bain slows the train for the scheduled stop at the switching yards. Within the maze of freight cars, Adams and Train 61 make a set-off, and in the coupling-up operation the crew finds six hoboes clinging to the hopper platforms. Although what the men are doing is illegal, the railroaders pay them no mind, and the freight lurches forward for the sandhill country of Monahans.

"They get a little wined up and aggravate you sometimes, but they've never given me any trouble," says Adams. "They're probably afraid of us, afraid we'll put 'em off. We carry some protection and they know we do. If they're trying to go somewhere I just let 'em ride. Now if they get on the engine I'll tell 'em they're not supposed to ride there. I've never had one refuse to get off."

But rear brakeman Moose Webb has not been so lucky. Back in 1947 he was trying to put a hobo off a slow-moving train in an industrial area when a savage confrontation ensued. He was forced to seek safety atop a boxcar, where a low-lying telephone line stretching across the track from a beer joint struck him, knocking him flat on the roof and inflicting a gash in his cheek requiring six stitches to close.

But that was far from the most dramatic event which has happened to Webb along the rails. In 1969 a piggyback came uncoupled from a locomotive and roared unchecked through the Big Spring switching yards. Burdened by rain gear, Webb raced to it, clutched the ladder, and hung on for dear life as he pulled the manual brake.

"I was scared when I caught it," he says, "but I stopped it before it got to the bumping post."

Shaken, Webb climbed the stairs into the depot and suddenly collapsed from a heart attack.

He was laid up six months, but even so, the incident did not leave him gun shy, and the rails beckoned as soon as he recovered.

Dwarf oaks crawl up and down a barrage of sand hills as Train 61 nears Monahans, and conductor Linus Tucker checks his invoices to see what the next set-offs will be. From his position in the caboose at the rear of the train, Tucker, more than six decades in age, is in sole charge of the freight cars he cannot even see. Today has been a good day for him; except for a problem with an air brake and a faulty electrical switch on an engine, everything has gone smoothly. But still he misses the time when coal-burners were in full steam, back when he first climbed aboard in 1939.

"It was the noise they made and the way they ran," he says in trying to explain his fascination with the engines of a bygone era. "Just like a child, I liked to hear an engine puff and blow."

"They had a different type of whistle, and there were passenger trains and wooden cabooses," adds Webb. "It was just a lot more exciting, a lot more enjoyable."

Things are different on the rails now, for all of them. They still like it, but not to the degree they once did.

"The diesel engine took all the damned glamour out of railroading," trainmaster Hanfeld says bluntly.

But these men who have found a lifelong affinity for the rails have remained. "If you stay for five years you'll never quit," says Adams. For the world of railroading has transcended a mere occupation for them; it has become a lifeblood flowing from the very heart of their families. Tucker's grandfather worked the railroad fifty-five years, his father fifty-two, his brother fifty-one, and an uncle thirty-three. Bain's son is a brakeman riding out of Big Spring. And Adams, who says his own son became fascinated with trains after he took him on a ride as a five-year-old, now has a fellow switchman bearing his last name.

It's been a long road for these men, one that's carried them enough miles to circle the globe forty times and one which will extend far beyond the getting-off point in Toyah. For to their last breaths the rails will go with them, bound to their souls as inseparably as coal car to steam locomotive.

Monahans receding, black smoke drifts back over the freight cars like a comforting blanket as Train 61 and its crew disappear into the horizon of the Pecos.

Boxcars and Brakies

Hoboes

$\mathcal{A}$ long the rails that cross the Pecos country lives a breed of lost, misguided men.

Hoboes. Vagrants. Transients. Tramps.

These are the men of a rough and tumble life amid weaving freight trains, noisy switching yards, and putrid hobo jungles, the men who lunge for ladders along swiftly moving boxcars and huddle against the blazing heat in open-topped gondolas. They are society's rejecters and rejected, the dropouts and misfit derelicts of America.

In a clan apart from the world and its ideologies, they live a skid-row life along the back alleys of the nation, the rail lines which for them have no hint of dignity or hope of destiny. Rather, the railroads hold the only things which matter to the outcasts: shining rails forming a gateway to the horizon and freights to carry them toward it. The lure of the unseen, the unknown is strong, and when they "swing a freight" to find refuge in a boxcar or on a piggyback, they are displaying as much a sense of direction as they perhaps ever will. They are both free and bound, knowing no other existence, wanting none.

They are men like Doyle, the "Mississippi Boy"; Johnny, nicknamed "Slim," hardly more than a kid; and Robert, the patriarch of the group, who labels every new bo he comes across with a moniker of his own design. Together they travel these forgotten roads of America, a breed separate, without purpose other than that provided by the tug of the locomotive on the freight cars or that bestowed by the bottle.

These are the men of lost weekends, lost lives spent submerged in booze or boxcars or the immense sea of mystery indwelling every man. And it shows.

They fight. They talk in vulgarities. They take jobs, lose them. The liquor clouds their thoughts, slurs their speech, racks their bodies. Their voiced future is a vague misconception of "another city waitin' somewhere down the line," and the next thing any of them know they are clinging to a fast freight headed toward it, the wind a gale in their faces and black diesel smoke drifting over the line of cars from the locomotive like a shroud.

The same things await them at every stop: Freight yards. Odd jobs. Sleeping in the open. Hovering over a fire beside the track. For the Mississippi Boy, Slim, and Robert it may never end, not until the booze destroys or they slip beneath the wheels or wake up in a boxcar to a knife at their throats. And the only reason any of them can give for riding the rails is Doyle's simplistic comment: "We take a wild hair and we go."

On this day, that is just what the Mississippi Boy is looking to do. He walks down the center of the Missouri Pacific track in Odessa, the summer sun ablaze on his bare chest as his scuffed boots crunch gravel between the ties. His dingy T-shirt is tucked through his belt and dangles along his hip, and dark curly hair edges from beneath the blue cap emblazoned "Kentucky Wildcats" twisted backward on his head. He turns from the rails, his frayed jeans rasping against weeds.

"You work on the train?" he asks as I approach from the freight yards. The voice is southern, distinctly accented, the tongue thickened by whiskey.

"No. You?"

"Nah." Doyle studies me carefully, and I return the stare. Mutual suspicion, mistrust, is common along the rails. Every bo is on his own. No one can be dependent and survive.

"I was wanting to catch one," I say.

The lines at Doyle's glazed eyes relax. "That's what we doin'. Me'n two other guys waitin' over there by the tracks. You headed our way, come on over'n join us."

They lie sprawled in the gravel beside the rails in the shade of Loop 338 overpass just east of the Odessa switching yards where a big freight is being coupled up. They are waiting for an "east-bounder." Only three days ago, they rolled into the city on the wheels of a freight, found a quick job operating a jackhammer at a construction site, and picked up a few bucks. Now, the green army surplus duffle bag filled with pork and beans, cigarettes, canned meat, Gatorade, and booze, they are looking to go back down the line.

"We come from the east and we headed east," Doyle says as I join them, squat on the gravel to look the group over.

Three men. The duffle bag. A frameless pack stuffed with gear. And an amber jug of Canadian Mist, one quart consumed, one quart sloshing inside, that binds them only as brothers of the bottle. For here, there are no brothers of the rails, no unification beyond that of mutual inebriation.

"Wherever we go, we go together," says Doyle. "We all together." But his attempt at camaraderie is lost in the squabbling over food, the frequent fights that seem to rule everyday life.

Robert raises himself to his elbow, extends a sweaty hand to me. "From Tennessee originally," he allows. The patriarch is forty-four or forty-five, shirtless, with gray-flecked hair and a tattoo of a skull and crossbones blackening his upper arm. Whiskey is strong on his breath and bits of gravel cling to his ribs. When he turns and reaches for the jug, twin tattoos of nudes reclined in champagne glasses dance at his shoulder blades.

"How long you been riding?" I ask.

He guzzles from the jug, the liquid dribbling from the corners of his mouth. He wipes it away with the back of his hand. "All my life," he says.

Johnny lies flat on his back a few feet from the rail, his sandy hair strewn across dirt and gravel. Unable to cope with the liquor, he has fallen asleep with his mouth open. The light mustache that rims his lip flutters when he exhales.

Doyle nudges him. "Hey, Johnny, we got us a eastbounder couplin' up." He does not awaken. The noise of autos rushing by on nearby U.S. 80 has no effect. Neither does the roar of the truck on the overpass above, its gears whining, screaming.

Johnny is just barely out of adolescence, nineteen, maybe twenty. His face is gaunt, reddened. Even when he will awaken in a few minutes, his speech, actions, will remain incoherent, for he is a product of the rails, a product of the bottle. And so it may be for the rest of his life.

"Me'n Johnny been together 'bout a month," says Doyle. "I been knowin' Robert here 'bout two weeks. We all together."

The Mississippi Boy is thirty-eight or forty, with hairy chest and muscular arms imprinted with tattoos. One mark is the embodiment of death, clothed in flowing black robe and brandishing a scythe. He is from Mississippi, he tells me, a certain pride filling his voice. Got a wife, an eighty-eight-acre farm. Kids? Five of 'em. Four in high school, one in elementary.

"If your wife's there, what are you doing here?" I ask.

It is the wrong question. Doyle becomes defensive, belligerent. "Gotta make ends meet," he snarls. "My wife, she knows, she accepts that. Ain't nobody to tell me I don't provide for my fam'ly." He takes the jug, drinks long and hard. "I provide for my fam'ly. Nobody gonna tell me I don't."

He glances around at a locomotive approaching from a side track, the wheels clattering over sections of polished rail. He rises, walks toward the moving cars. A brakeman drops from a hopper ladder as the locomotive jerks, screeches to a stop.

"Hey buddy, this train goin' east?"

The brakeman nods, giving arm signals to the engineer.

"How long?"

"I'd say about an hour."

"You got any boxcars on here? How 'bout a pig'back?"

"I don't think so. Y'all can walk down the line, see what you can find. It's pretty hot. Best thing for y'all to do is find a spot in the shade and wait a while."

The railroad employee is friendly, even obliging, but it is a friendliness born of suspicion, fear. There are no "tough cops and brakemen" who tell Mississippi Boy he cannot ride, no "bulls" with shotguns or paddy wagons. In fact, says Doyle, in all his years on the rails "they ain't nobody *ever* bothered me. The only ones ever bothered me was the city po-leese. They ran a check on me. They checked me out on bein' a migrant. But I ain't ever done nothin', so they let me alone."

Doyle pulls Johnny to his feet. The younger man wakes up cursing, his speech indistinct. "What the *hail* ya want?" he demands.

"Come on, Johnny. We got us a eastbounder. We gonna go find us a car to climb in."

The hoboes stagger through a world of booze down the line of freight cars, past the hoppers, the gondolas, the tankers. There are no boxcars on this train, repeats the Mississippi Boy. But it's traveling east. That's good enough, ain't it?

"Where y'all headed?" I ask.

"The East Coast," says Doyle, toting the heavy duffle bag as his boots slip, grind against gravel. "Corpus. The East Coast by way of Corpus. We get us a job down there."

The job in Odessa is over. For now. But it's not the first time. He's no stranger to the freight yards on the outskirts of the city. "Been here lotsa times," he says. He may be back. In time. But Corpus is waiting down the line. A day here, a couple there, and the rails beckon again. It can be no other way, not for the Mississippi Boy.

Ever hitchhike? He shrugs. "If they ain't no other way. But it's kinda hard, bein' there's three of us."

The rails are no respecters of numbers. Or of lost lives. So they are here, where hoboes are a vanishing breed of homeless men, strangely contrasted with the illegal aliens who ride only in search of a better home.

They finally decide on a yellow and black gondola, an open-roofed car exposed to the scorching sun. One by one we climb the outside ladder, the grimy rungs soiling our palms. It is sweltering inside. The metal of the floor and five-foot walls absorbs the heat of the afternoon sun, radiates it to bake skin. They curse the heat, curse the train for not carrying a boxcar. Cursing leads to bickering. Robert ambles to the far end, urinates in the corner. Meanwhile, Doyle, seeking what little breeze there is, takes a seat atop the juncture of the walls. "You SOB," says Robert, upon turning. "We ain't gonna have none of that. If we're gonna be down here you get your butt down here with us."

Johnny has become nauseous. He pulls himself up, leans over the rim, vomits to the track. No one asks what is wrong.

After twenty minutes the gondola's heat, accentuated by the booze, has become unbearable. Johnny has collapsed across the duffle bag, his head bent, one arm twisted awkwardly beneath him. Saliva trickles from his mouth.

Doyle hums a song. He says it's "Mississippi Freight Train Blues." Robert pokes him in the shoulder. "Too damned hot in here, Mississippi Boy. How much longer till that hour's up?"

Doyle glances at the watch on his browned arm. "This thing prob'ly won't start movin' 'fore four o'clock," he opines.

They decide to leave the gear inside, wait below in the shade of a tank car along the parallel side track. I descend first, planting a boot on the coupling and swinging down. Doyle drops a water jug to me, then the Gatorade and the ever-lightening bottle of whiskey. Robert climbs down, stands beside me as Doyle tries to rouse Johnny. The kid does not respond for a long while.

"What you suppose is wrong with him?" I ask Robert.

He shrugs. "Hell, there ain't no tellin'," he says. "I don't think Mississippi Boy's gonna let Slim hobo with us no more."

Johnny finally awakens, cursing indiscriminately. He swings a leg over the rim, the soiled sneakers seeking a rung. He totters on the brink, makes it halfway down with loosened muscles. He loses his grip, crumples to the rail, his back colliding with the iron coupling. He groans. Only I move to help him; the others simply wander away. He is on his own here, and is incapable of dealing with it.

We sit on the rail beneath the tank car and breathe the exhaust fumes drifting from Highway 80; the acrid current mixes with the odor of liquor and leaves a foul taste in our mouths. They curse one another, become belligerent. No one seems to know why, or cares. Doyle, his eyes narrowed, fists clenched, stands up menacingly before Johnny. Johnny levels an epithet at him. Doyle shoves him in the chest; Johnny staggers back and falls hard to the gravel.

"You two gotta fight it out right now," says Robert, rising.

Johnny turns his epithets on Robert.

"Don't call me that, you SOB," snarls the patriarch. "I'll cut your damned head off."

Tension reigns for long seconds; real violence seems a certainty to me. Finally the brotherhood of the bottle takes over again. They sit down, drink, and drink some more. Johnny and Robert shake hands. "You'n me, we ran that jackhammer, didn't we?" comments Johnny.

"Yeah," says Robert.

"We ran it good, didn't we?"

"Yeah," says Robert. Liquor runs down his chin.

"We all together now," says Doyle, drinking from the jug, passing it on. "Ever'thing we do, we do together."

A shrill whistle pierces the air. The train begins to move, wheels grinding against track and clicking at rail joints. One at a time they grasp the rungs, feeling the tug of the train as it pulls them from the gravel. The movement gives a feeling of power, a sense of freedom. The ties sweep down the track beneath the coupling in ever-quickening rhythm, becoming a blur. Diesel smoke drifts over the gondola, stings eyes. The roar of the wheels climbs upward through metal floor into boots, batters legs.

The freight yards recede, disappear beyond a half-mile of iron and wood and steel pummeling over railroad. Odessa is a memory now. It was home for three days. The construction site, the quick bucks, the freight yards, it's all behind them now.

And the horizon looms forever ahead, never quite attainable, not for these men who must live—and die—along the rails of America.

Hobo Bill

*T*he men who frequent the Road to Nowhere sometimes find in the rails and crossties of the railroad lines of the Pecos country a quality that soothes the wanderlust in their souls.

The road is a rough one for many, a dead end in a boxcar or a bottle of cheap wine or under the wheels. But for Bill, it has become the road to self-discovery.

In his three and a half decades Bill has experienced the highs and lows of life, known satisfaction and endured agony. A North Carolina native, he went to college two years, served eight years with the Seabees, and twice survived enemy slugs in his body during two hitches in Vietnam. He was a settled family man, his life firmly entrenched in his home.' He had a wife, three children, a comfortable place to live, and a steady job that offered financial security. Then the tragedy of a car wreck took it all from him in an instant, and he was left alone.

It drove him to the rails, stirred within him man's unquenchable longing for that which he cannot ever grasp. And in ten years' time he has not looked back.

The tragedy would have forever disillusioned a lesser man, spawned an aimless, broken shell of a person, racked with bitterness, wallowing in the mire of self-pity. But not with Bill, whose bo moniker is a colorful, though uncharacteristic, "Wild Bill." He learned to cope—as he had to or die—and found his own meaning in the rails, where everyday life bespeaks a simpler era in which the biggest worry is catching the next westbound freight.

It is vital on this morning in the Odessa freight yards. A night on the town in a local bar has depleted his funds. The blood bank

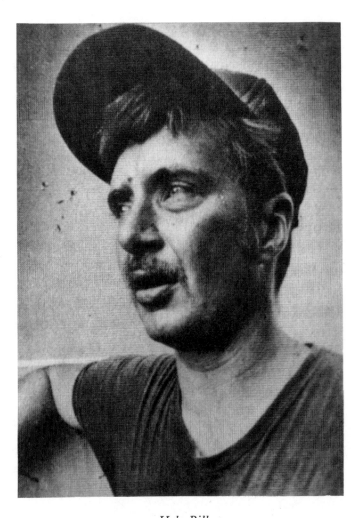

Hobo Bill

and a quick ten bucks are waiting down the line in El Paso, and
beyond that, the alfalfa fields ready for harvest in Elko, Nevada.

It is nine-thirty, and Bill, white tote bag in lap, reclines with
shoulders resting against the wheel of a truck trailer on a "piggyback"—a flat car—within the half-mile maze of hallways formed
of gravel and rails and several hundred freight cars. These yards

are known to be safe, where boes are free from harassment by railroad detectives or "bulls," and Bill and his long-time hoboing companion, The Quiet One, have been waiting for a train since four-thirty a.m.

A stoutly built man, not tall, Bill sports a sandy mustache, while blond hair edges out from beneath a maroon cap that says "Take this Job and Shove It." But it's the small silvery cross dangling from his neck that seems as out-of-place on a self-confessed "tramp" as Bill's demeanor does to the sometimes brutal and demanding life along the tracks.

He speaks with an assured politeness. His words are carefully chosen, void of the rambling quality and choice epithets that fill the conversation of many of his peers. The eyes, as blue as a deep spring pool, indicate great intelligence, foresight.

And he is a devout Christian.

"I've been in the church all my life," he says. "The Assembly of God. You meet some tramps that are religious, some that aren't. I've met a preacher that travels these rails, preaches at hobo jungles." He glances at the cross against his dark T-shirt. "My grandmother gave it to me when I first started tramping. She told me it'll always keep you alive on the tracks and keep you safe. My grandfather was an old-time hobo and he always wore one, and it took care of him."

Thus far, it has done its job. Despite the dangers of life along the rails, he has not been injured. But there have been some scares. A couple of times he has come close to getting thrown beneath the wheels when he's lunged for freight car ladders.

"I've jumped 'em when they're moving so fast it's slung me around, slammed my legs into the side, and bounced me off the gravel," he remembers. "But the hardest thing to do is get *off* a moving freight. The best way is to hold on to the ladder and start running, and when you can keep up, let go."

Even the night before offered its own dangers. The Quiet One, a cotton-headed man of sixty-three so named "because I don't have much to say," sprawls on the piggyback nursing an ugly bruise along his right jaw, a souvenir from a fight outside an Odessa bar after they worked a couple of days in the city.

"'Bout knocked my teeth in," he whispers, adjusting his sweaty western hat. His face carries the wrinkles of the four decades he's spent on the rails "getting from Point A to Point B" since his early years in Colorado.

"We were spending our money around pretty freely in there," says Bill, puffing on a cigarette. "They thought they needed it worse than we did. Just some young punks. They found out we weren't as easy to run off as they thought we'd be."

Down the track a locomotive couples up with the line of freight cars and the piggyback jerks forward with a screech. Bill and The Quiet One grab their tote bags, drop to the gravel. "I was just starting to get comfortable," says Bill.

The legs of his khaki-colored jeans rasp together as he walks down the narrow corridor, walled on one side by the moving freight and on the other by the stilled hoppers and tankers. "They all know me up and down the tracks as 'Wild Bill,'" he allows, and when he slings his gear across his back, proof of his moniker becomes apparent in the sketch on his tanned forearm.

But beyond his display of numerous tattoos and his talk of "drinking cheap wine" to replenish his blood, little in his deportment identifies him with the typical hobo, if such an entity exists. He is neither an outcast nor a reject, but rather uses the freights for transportation from job to job. Like many of the derelicts he comes across, he hits the blood banks "two or three times a week" for quick cash and sleeps in boxcars or hobo jungles, but it is purely a matter of convenience, not of addiction. He might as easily be wearing a three-piece suit in a downtown office building or, at the least, find ample income operating heavy equipment.

Whether or not the rails will shape the rest of his life is of no concern to him, and the potential stability of a permanent home and steady employment thus far has failed to lure him away from the freedom of the rails.

"*This* is our home," interjects The Quiet One, nodding to the freight cars.

But Bill's comment is more profound. "I've had that once," he says quietly, his eyes reflecting memories of his home, his career. "When I got out of the Seabees after eight years, all I got was a pat on the back. Then I lost my wife and three kids in a car wreck and decided to take off, travel. Now, I don't worry about the future. This time next week I hope to be sitting in Elko, Nevada."

Houston last week, El Paso tomorrow, Elko in a few days. That's as much an itinerary as he cares to formulate. But even at that, he refuses to be bound by preordained routes, destinations. "Who knows," he philosophizes, only half in jest, "I may get to drinking that cheap wine in El Paso and hear a train coming by and go out and catch one going the wrong way."

The "right way" for transients during late spring, he says, is west, where employment looms in the Nevada hay fields. Bill already has a job lined up in Elko, where he will operate baling equipment. It won't be his first trip to Nevada, nor is this his maiden run through Odessa. For he has ridden the rails "from one end of the United States to the other" in the ten years since the night he hopped his first freight at the urging of liquor and a buddy.

He and The Quiet One came down from Oregon to Houston a year ago, and after two or three months in the alfalfa fields they may follow the tracks back up to the Northwest, where the chill of winter will keep them off the freights.

Hoboing is a rough life, and many tramps are on their own, unable or unwilling to depend on anyone else. But Wild Bill and The Quiet One have found in each other kindred souls. Although the previous five years have spawned "a few disagreements, even a couple of fights" between the two, "we always get over it," says Bill. "We look out for each other. We're both vets, and if one of us gets sick he goes to the VA hospital, and the other one will hang around town till he gets out."

A dull roar echoes up the corridor of freight cars to the east, gradually increasing in intensity until a shrill whistle defines its source.

"There she is!" cries The Quiet One, watching between coupled tankers as the westbounder thunders by, its wheels clattering across sections of rail.

They climb across the coupling, drop to the gravel, face the moving train. The Quiet One eyes a piggyback, loaded with a truck trailer, sweeping toward him at ten miles per hour. He takes off sprinting in the gravel, tosses his tote bag onto the car, and grasps the ladder.

Bill is at his shoulder, throwing his gear up, lunging for the rungs. The momentum of the train pulls him from the ground, leaves the wind a storm in his face. He is westbound now. The blood bank is just down the line, and next week, perhaps, there will be Elko. Beyond that, well, he will wait and see.

Once his future was set, entwined with the lives of his wife and children. There was no Road to Nowhere, no road to self-discovery that needed traveling. But that was then, when the rails held for him only vague curiosity, passing thoughts, a world of misconceptions.

Now, they hold his destiny.

Hobo Bill

The Border

ĸȣ

$\mathcal{T}$he river.

Mexican nationals call it *Rio Bravo del Norte*.

To Americans, it is the Rio Grande.

It separates one country from another, one *world* from another, and in that respect is both as narrow as a few yards and as broad as untold ages.

And every night, it harbors a life and death struggle.

Arnold P. accelerates a camouflage-green vehicle down the highway and glances at the city of Del Rio and United States Border Patrol Sector Headquarters disappearing in the rear view mirror. Ahead lies remote borderland ruled by sagebrush and a late afternoon summer sun, and soon this man who wears the uniform of *la Verde* (the Green) will search its hidden places for illegal aliens. Those he finds may level at him a more vicious name—*Perro!* (Dog). But he has a job to do, that of guarding the United States border against illegal entry, and the ugly scar above his left elbow is a constant reminder that this game is a deadly one. Six months ago Arnold and his partner, responding to data relayed by a seismic detector along the Rio Grande, came upon four illegal immigrants armed with rifles. The aliens fired and ran back across the river. One slug ripped through Arnold's arm. He never knew who shot him or why.

Arnold was back on the job in a few weeks, patrolling those same banks. The experience left him more cautious, but still without animosity.

"I think they know we're not going to harm them," he says as the highway stripes disappear rhythmically beneath the left fender. "They're not afraid of us. They just don't want to get caught, that's all. But if we didn't try to stop 'em, everybody in Mexico would be over here." His partner, Iowa native Gary N., nods in agreement from the passenger's seat.

Twenty miles southeast of Del Rio, Arnold pulls off the highway, the tires slinging gravel, and stops at a ranch gate. The rancher, acquiescing to a law which allows the Border Patrol access to holdings within twenty-five miles of the river, has provided a key. Beyond the gate, the agents speed along a gravel and dirt road in backcountry bearing sage, prickly pear, and mesquites scorched by the desert heat. On either side lie occasional evidences of migrant traffic: blackened fire rings, tin cans, plastic jugs. For in this ranch's mile and a half of river frontage, five shallow areas have been identified as illegal crossings and now hold seismic or magnetic detectors to warn immigration officials of entries.

But the nightfall that likely will see the devices triggered is still an hour away, so as Arnold and Gary near the river they halt and creep toward a line of mesquites shielding the initial crossing, one hundred yards distant. The lenses of their binoculars glint in the sunlight which streams through the gnarled, thin-leaved limbs. The crossing is empty. For now. When they turn toward their car, leather holsters bearing their .357 magnums creak and Gary readjusts the earphone of the portable radio which keeps him in contact with headquarters and data relayed by detectors.

A couple of miles upstream, where a high bluff sentinels rippled water and Mexican lowlands, Arnold stops the vehicle a second time and the pair stalks the crossing through yellowed grass shrouded by overhanging mesquite limbs. Exiting from the brush in open view of the opposite bank, they crawl quickly through double barbed-wire fences erected against diseased Mexican livestock and slither on their bellies down a trench to a jutting point of the bluff. Here, thorny limbs lie stacked at the base of a lone mesquite which clings precariously to the rim of the thirty-foot precipice. In a sandy hollow before the blind they sprawl and peer at the crossing beyond.

Border patrolmen Arnold and Gary study brush bordering the Rio Grande for signs of illegal aliens.

It is almost dusk. The sun is sinking slowly into the gleaming river to the west. Below, an animal nickers, and a dozen Mexican horses wade into the shallows to drink. Oddly, the terrain unfurls green behind them, but the flood plain deceives; the horizon holds only desolation. But for the dull roar of a vehicle testifying to the presence of an adobe village two miles downstream, it would seem without human presence.

Arnold lifts, then lowers, his binoculars. He nudges Gary and nods at two Mexicans who approach a dirt stock tank a hundred yards inland on the Mexican side. Each wears a *sombrero*, and one carries a bottle of *tequila*. Oblivious to the watching eyes, they walk to the river at a point at which a mesquite thicket fringes the ripples. Guzzling from the bottle, they survey the shallows and the bluff beyond for several minutes before retreating to the security of the dry earthen tank.

It is not yet dark enough to cross, and a waiting game ensues. The Mexicans wait for night to blanket the river, and the border patrolmen for their quarry's first steps onto American soil. It is a familiar scenario to Arnold and Gary; they generally spend most of the night crouched behind this blind, or another like it. To an outsider, it all seems a well-staged play: look, wait, capture, return them to Mexico so a day or two later everyone can give an encore performance.

On this evening, the border patrolmen patiently hold their position an hour. Then Gary suddenly lowers his binoculars and cups a hand over the radio earphone. He pokes Arnold and reaches for his hat. "Two hits—zero thirty."

Arnold drops his binoculars to dangle at his neck and the two are up, sprinting up the trench, clawing through the fences, dodging the mesquites. Seismic instruments have detected two intruders on the American bank at the first crossing. There, Mexican nationals have just become illegal aliens, and Arnold and Gary must forget the two below the bluff who played a waiting game and won.

Unilluminated limbs slap against fenders as Gary drives down the road at breakneck speed. A deer bounds across, shadowy and swift, and as the car explodes out of a mesquite thicket a moment later the border patrolmen spot two upright silhouettes fifty yards away.

Gary slams on the brakes, slowing just long enough to determine which direction they'll flee. They remain stationary, and he accelerates the vehicle onward to skid it to a halt at their feet. Arnold is out into the storm of dust before the car is fully stopped, and within seconds he has confronted the aliens.

Neither tries to run. They are either too old or too tired. They only stand stoically with packs under arms and answer the questions posed them in Spanish. One is in his late forties, with deeply terraced face and tightly drawn cheeks. A thin mustache rims his upper lip—and the lip is quivering from realization that his hopes, indeed the hopes of perhaps his entire family, have been shattered.

The other man is younger, in his late twenties, though his features already are lined and leathery from years of toil beneath the deadly Mexican sun. Like his companion, he wears leggings of cardboard from boot tops to knees to fend off the fangs of the rattler.

At Gary's instructions, they lay their packs on the ground and open them. They carry only a change of clothes, tortillas, water, and a few cans of food. They say they are from Guanajuato, six hundred miles deep in Mexico. Pooling their resources, they bought bus tickets and rode northward to a border village, then waited for nightfall and crossed over. When Arnold asks where they were going, they reply in Spanish, "To find work, wherever we could."

As the border patrolmen escort them to the patrol car for the long ride back to headquarters, a strange irony settles over the scene: The two Mexicans left homes and hungry families to travel six hundred miles in search of a fair chance in life, yet attained only one hundred yards into the country of that hope before falling.

Inside the vehicle, the four occupants sit quietly as the river recedes into the night. Yet it never disappears, not even when the lights of Del Rio glitter against the horizon.

It binds these men, this river, holding them in center stage of a never-ending drama. Yet at the same time, it separates, damning two of them to the cast of a tragedy.

And only the inscrutable hand of fate decides who plays which roles.

In the Border Patrol "Game"

※

*T*o Charles H., his job is just like the majority of jobs: "You either know it or you don't."

Charles knows his. He is a United States Border Patrol agent stationed in Big Spring, and he has learned through years of experience how to look at a brown-skinned person and ascertain if it would be worthwhile to check for papers.

His stubby fingers fold themselves across the steering wheel as he drives a Border Patrol vehicle across a north Midland housing development with red dirt as choppy as a stormy sea. Silvery handcuffs dangle from the gear shift and bang against the steering column in staccato fashion, then cease to clatter as tires jump a curb to find pavement.

Charles stops and nods at the wire and steel of a building form, and in the dark shades that veil his eyes from the late winter sun one worker becomes reflected. He is young, eighteen or twenty, with white-kneed jeans and red T-shirt barely concealing his rib cage. He stands half-leaned on a shovel, his stubbly chin buried into the bend of his sweaty elbow. He looks up long enough to catch the green of *la Verde* and then casually lowers his eyes to the shovel tip.

"That one there looks like an alien," the forty-year-old border patrolman says in a deep drawl between slurps on the gum that leaves the sickly sweet odor of snuff in the air. "Don't know why the other unit didn't check him."

"What makes you think he's from Mexico?" I ask.

He turns his palms over in a shrug. "Well, it's just one of those things you learn to tell in this bus'ness. The people, they act diff'rent, they dress diff'rent, they just refuse to look at ya. You can pass a truckload on the street and you can tell they're illegals 'cause they won't be lookin' at ya—they'll look straight ahead, off to the side, any place but right at ya. This one sure looks like he's from Mex'co. Let's find out."

He keys the radio mike and contacts another unit, concealed by the skeletons of upgoing homes. "Say, you check this'n in the red cap and red shirt?" he asks.

"Ten-four. He's got an I-one-five-one [legal resident alien card]."

Charles places the mike back in the clip and nods. "I figgered he was from Mex'co," he comments, feeling the edges of the brown handlebar mustache that droops at the corners of his mouth. "Got his work papers though."

Charles is a total professional at his job, all right, even if he does seem cast in the Slim Pickens mold—complete with good ol' boy humor pouring forth from beneath the John L. Sullivan mustache in a nasal twang that leaves off the closing "G's" and slurs syllables to create distinctly West Texan words like "reg'lar" and "op'ration." And too, there is something about the leathery face and broad shoulders which, while adding sinew to his six-foot-two frame even when sagging slightly at the USBP patch, arouse memories of the late actor.

But to his fellow agents he's just plain "Charlie," a nickname he doesn't like but "suffers with purty reg'lar." But like the "sayin'," he adds through a half grin, "I don't care what they call me, long as they call me at eatin' time."

As he engages in a "normal day's work" in checking construction sites for illegal aliens, Charles reflects on his career with the Border Patrol and offers personal insight into the deluge of Mexican nationals into the Pecos country.

And when it's brought down to humanitarian terms, Charles —not surprisingly for someone so enmeshed in the issue—is able to display a measure of empathy for those he pursues, as though he realizes most are not criminals but poor persons seeking survival for themselves and their families.

An intense irony, in fact, pervades Charles's situation. For when he discusses his job and his own family it becomes obvious that while he and an illegal alien are diametrically opposed in "The Game," each is ruled by much the same desires and dreams.

"I love my job—it's the greatest thing that ever happened to me," he says, but at the same time he makes it clear that the real importance of his career is that it "feeds my wife and puts my girl through school." And so the very cause which allows his family to survive is the same which, paradoxically, is depriving others of the same opportunity, or at least placing an added burden on them. He admits readily that had fate led his wife, his nineteen-year-old daughter, and him to be born Mexican nationals, he would be in the United States too "till they put me in jail—and not knowin' any more'n I do, I'd probably still come back even then."

He pauses to look across the seat at me and his brow becomes ridged in seriousness. "As long as there's a disparity between these two economies, these people'll be over here. Let's face it—if you were down there, you'd be over here, and if I was down there I'd be over here." And it is this awareness, more than any inherent compassion, that brings him to treat the illegal aliens whom he apprehends with respect and dignity.

Charles, who first began wearing the insignia of the Border Patrol and strapping its official weapon—a .357 magnum—at his hip fourteen years ago, started out in law enforcement as a Department of Public Safety trooper. He moved on to a position as a city policeman in Littlefield, and then pursuit of financial stability for his wife and young daughter led him to sign up with the Border Patrol.

"I turned twenty-six on a December thirty-first and started in on January second," he recalls. "I was sent to the academy [in Port Isabel] in the winter, and I moved my wife into a little tourist court down there behind an orange grove." His family since has

In the Border Patrol "Game"

followed him to El Centro, California, and the Texas cities of Pecos, Big Spring, and Eagle Pass, and then back to Big Spring when he became supervisor of the regional station.

At a north Midland construction site, Charles stops the van beside stacks of lumber and watches through a chain-link fence as his fellow officers take an illegal alien into custody. The man, in his late thirties with blue cap and soiled hands, offers no resistance, only calm acceptance of his fate. As the agents escort him to the construction office to "clean him up"—Border Patrol jargon for allowing him to collect his wages and belongings—I ask Charles if it is uncommon for an illegal alien to go along so peaceably.

When he begins talking in detail about his job and the exact procedure following apprehension of illegal immigrants, the impression surfaces that it is indeed all just a game, one without ultimate victors. He apprehends them in the ten counties patrolled by his Big Spring station, then within only hours, or days at most, an Immigration and Naturalization Service bus transports them to Ojinaga, where directly across the Rio Grande they "get out and go their merry way."

Their "merry way," more often than not, is right back across the river into the United States, once they feel safely harbored by darkness against apprehension by *la Migra*. In a few days' time the very same illegal aliens may be working the identical construction or oilfield sites, without losing as much as a week's pay.

"That's the way it's played," Charles says, nodding. "When we put them in the back of the van they're us'lly singin' and whistlin'—they know they'll be back."

A telling example of the apparent folly of this game, he says, occurred several years ago when he picked up an illegal alien on a Friday afternoon in Dallas. The man was processed and flown to El Paso that night, then released across the international bridge in Juarez.

"Well," says Charles, shaking his head, "he grabbed a freight train comin' outa Chihuahua and I caught him comin' through Big

Spring on a boxcar Sunday mornin'. He said he didn't wanna miss a day of work."

Despite charges by some factions that his may be a useless job, Charles has a different outlook. "I don't feel that way at all," he says. He nods to a two-story brick structure as the van again speeds down a Midland thoroughfare. "I feel like if we weren't out here, they'd be stacked up as high as that wall over there."

But even so, he says, he is aware that his station barely skims the surface.

"We'd like to have a lot more efficient op'ration, but we come up here and have ten counties and just me'n those two men to work 'em," he says. "That's 2,250 square miles per man, and we're one short right now." He takes a deep breath and readjusts his position behind the steering wheel. "Needless to say, we don't go down ever' little road. We don't have enough men, and see that mileage on this truck? That 49,000 should have a *one* before it."

He slings a gnarled hand toward the grillwork that separates the cab from the detention area behind. "We only got seven seats back there and us'lly just one unit workin'. The objective when you leave the office ever' mornin' is to fill that truck up."

The other van stops at a residential construction site, and Charles watches as a fellow officer talks with a young man sitting atop the cab of a pickup. Upon returning to his unit the officer keys the mike and his voice crackles over the radio. "We were a little bit late on that one, Charlie—there's six pair of rubber boots [for concrete work] sittin' over there and nobody to wear 'em."

Charles shrugs it off and drives on, as though a feeling of complacency is commonplace in his vocation. "This is a very relaxed job; there's nothin' pressin' about it," he drawls. "Maybe one of our guilts is that we take the easy ones. It doesn't make sense to wear ourselves out one place when there's more right down the road. And those we miss here today, they'll still be here tomorrow."

He nods toward a skyscraper looming against the Midland horizon. "There's illegals all over that thing up there, but you never saw so much trouble in your life as you'd have once you tried

In the Border Patrol "Game"

gettin' 'em down. One time we got after this illegal and he crawled out on the end of one of those cranes. You never saw anybody as scared as he was, or us either when we went out after him. We didn't enjoy it much, but we got him."

Danger, though, is a rarity in his profession, says Charles, as long as "we don't get careless." His index finger never has squeezed the trigger of his .357 magnum in the line of duty, and when asked how often he has drawn his weapon, he merely shakes his head. However, there have been occasions in which he has found himself in potentially lethal situations.

A few years ago while stationed along the border at Eagle Pass, he recalls, he and another unit got involved in high-speed pursuit of a supposed alien smuggler who kept crashing into *la Verde's* patrol cars and knocking them off the road. Charles's vehicle reached speeds of 120 miles per hour during the chase, which ended when the smuggler's engine blew up and became engulfed in flames, shrouding the roadway in smoke. "Me'n the other border patrolman ran right through it and somehow we switched positions on the road," Charles remembers with a grin. "I was leadin' him goin' in, and when we came outa there he was leadin' me." The smuggler, meanwhile, had abandoned his fiery vehicle and was apprehended along with seven San Salvadoran women.

While the Border Patrol is Charles's profession, it is not his life, and when he turns fifty he plans on "checkin' it to 'em" and moving on to "bigger and better things, like fishin' and sleepin'-in in the mornin's."

But for now, more building sites loom ahead. He stops and assists his officers in escorting another undocumented worker into the van. The foreman comes up. "Aren't you the one that stopped our truck last week and picked up the same man?" he asks of the Big Spring supervisor.

The foreman is partially right. The Mexican national had told Charles on that occasion that his wife was living in Midland, so the border patrolman had carried him home and filed papers allowing them three days to leave the country. "He was back on the job in an hour," says the foreman.

Charles nods. "We'll take him with us this time," he promises.

Inside the van the Mexican national eases back in the seat and stares through the window at the construction site. He knows he'll be bused back to Ojinaga, which likely will keep him off the job a week this time instead of an hour.

As for Charles, well, he has more sites to check "down the road" and more illegal aliens to apprehend. He knows his job, all right—even if it is just part of a game.

The Illegal Women

The fear lives in their eyes, and betrays itself in each nervous shift toward the slightest disturbance.

It lives too in their frames, as they squirm uneasily despite soft-backed chairs and suddenly stiffen at the shrill blast of a passing siren.

They are illegal Mexican aliens who reside in Midland, and the fear of apprehension follows them, encompasses their thoughts, every day of their lives.

Irma, thirty-six and of medium build, wears a simple cotton dress with a flowery pattern of blue and white. Large-framed glasses rest on the ridge of her nose, and if she smiles at all, it only barely creases the corners of her mouth.

Her sister Elfida is thirty, with black hair fixed in a bun and eyes half-veiled by glasses. Less browned than Irma and more responsive in her facial features, she somehow finds the courage to smile frequently and even laugh in the face of a life filled with abuse, anxiety, and the uncertainty of what the next moment may bring.

Irma, her husband, and their five children have lived in concealment for two years in *los Estados Unidos*—the United States. Her husband makes good wages in his job as a floorman, roughneck, in the oil fields of the Permian Basin. Back home in Ojinaga, Mexico, he earned only one-seventh as much, and it came at the expense of long hours in the fields beneath the blazing sun. Ojinaga, directly across the Rio Grande from Presidio, is infamous for its devastating heat, strength-sapping rays, and scant rainfall.

Even the U.S. Border Patrol has a measure of empathy for their situation, and that of others like them. The sisters cannot understand, though, why the immigration service "drags people like us away from our homes" here in the United States. But it is obvious from talking with Irma and Elfida that their greatest enemy is not *la Migra*—the Border Patrol—but themselves. For the anxiety known to all illegal aliens can destroy as well as rule.

For a long while, Irma and Elfida have harbored the hope of becoming American citizens, with all the rights and privileges bestowed by the Constitution. Their mother, according to a Catholic Church baptismal record, was born in Barstow, Texas, and it was on this basis that an older brother received citizenship.

But only a half-week prior to their interview with me, these women saw their hopes dashed, and those of their husbands and children as well.

Traveling to the Immigration and Naturalization Service office in Dallas, the sisters presented the document detailing their mother's birthplace. INS officials gave them only a "fourth preference" rating—for which legal proceedings reportedly are backlogged four and a half years—and told them they must be out of the country in four days or be subject to deportation by the Border Patrol.

Midland is their home. They live and work and raise families there, pay taxes and spend their money in city stores. They would not leave as ordered. Instead, they would hide.

"We will make every effort to go from one area to another, continue changing addresses to keep *la Migra* from finding us," says Elfida in Spanish. One sees in their eyes they have little choice, unless returning to the abject poverty and hopelessness of Ojinaga is a choice.

Elfida has one other legal ground for avoiding her immediate return to Mexico. She is asking the INS to delay her voluntary deportation because of illness. The mental strain born of constant fear and the realization that her dreams of becoming an American citizen have been shattered have taken their toll on her. This, she hopes, will allow her time to seek alternatives through an attorney. But a problem exists. Attorneys require "a tremendous amount of money, which we do not have," she says, frustration carving lines into her forehead.

Elfida's son, almost two, was born on American soil, which automatically makes him a citizen exempt from deportation. And so a strange irony pervades her situation—her mother reportedly was born in Texas, and her son for certain, and yet because fate led her parents south of the *Rio Bravo del Norte* for the moment of her birth, she is an illegal alien with fourth preference status, wanted and hunted by the U.S. Border Patrol.

The American saga of a family unwanted and uncared for by its own nation began for Irma along a remote stretch of countryside between Presidio and Lajitas, where the muddy waters of the Rio Grande turn golden in the desert sun as they churn through awesome gorges flanked by sheer bluffs and towering pinnacles. Irma and her children long had awaited this day, for they had been separated many months from her husband, who had journeyed into *los Estados Unidos* to help them survive. He had provided for them all right, at the expense of blisters on his hands and the sacrifice of his own physical, emotional, and spiritual needs, but all the material things in the world cannot replace the love and caring of a husband and father.

And so it was that nightfall found a man, his wife, and their children ranging in age from three to fifteen carefully approaching on foot the rippling river from the creosote and sotol along the Mexican shore. They were quiet, wary, afraid. They knew *la Migra* watched the river closely and even had devices that detected a person's footsteps. But they were determined not to be victimized by the same pitfalls into which other would-be *mojados* (illegal aliens) sometimes plunge in seeking a fair chance in life. They had arranged for an American citizen to drive their car from Ojinaga across the international bridge to Presidio and downstream to Redford, Texas, where it awaited them that very moment.

From the carrizo and seep willow on the Mexican bank a small rowboat carrying mother, father, and five children eased into the river. The boat was cramped, and as a single paddle stirred gentle whirlpools, the water sloshed near the gunwales. The river was not wide here, perhaps thirty yards, and yet in a way it seemed a span beyond comprehension.

The mountains and cliffs painted against the nocturnal veil ahead looked no different than those behind. The sky seemed jeweled with the same stars, the earth strewn with the same desert vegetation. The air tasted no better, no worse, than that receding aft, and yet all because the river signified the imaginary boundary between one nation and another, one way of life and another, once they set foot on the opposite shore they would have committed a crime against the most powerful of countries.

Although once before, Irma's husband had been captured by *la Migra,* on this night they were not to be denied. They reached the American bank safely, climbed into their car, and drove away into the new hope that indwelt the dark horizon beyond the *Camino del Rio.* They were *mojados,* all of them, from the smallest child to the oldest man. And a life of constant anxiety awaited them.

Irma's husband found farm work in Kermit and later in Morton, before the promise of higher wages lured them to Midland. Elfida and her husband already were in the United States, having crossed over similarly at Redford and labored in Andrews before the demand for construction workers attracted them to Midland.

And even though a job as a heavy equipment operator at a downtown construction site was readily available for Elfida's husband, exploitation of him is evident, she claims with expressionistic gestures.

"He's underpaid because he's illegal," she says, explaining he makes only a little above minimum wage operating a loader. "The legals who do the same work make more." She admits, however, that company benefits are good, providing for insurance and vacation—something unheard of in the Ojinagan fields.

Elfida says her husband also suffered abuse at the hands of *la Migra* once when he crossed over and was captured. She cringes when she remembers, and says she asked him not to tell her all the details, as it tormented her too much. All she will say is, "*La Migra* got their dogs after him and he was bitten while they were chasing him."

It was a bad experience for her husband, and for her. She hopes it never happens again, but she never knows what the next day will bring her family.

And this uncertainty is the hardest element to bear. She realizes every morning when her husband leaves for work that it may be the last time she sees him for a long while, or forever. With realistic awareness of their dilemma, Elfida and her husband have worked out a plan should a Border Patrol raid claim him.

"Anytime he's not home by eight p.m., I'm supposed to pick the car up from work, because I'll know he's been captured," she explains quietly.

But even in consideration of the most serious calamity, she is able to grasp a measure of humor. "One time he had to work till ten, and I had a heart attack because I thought *la Migra* had taken him." She smiles, but only in bittersweet fashion.

Their plan is even more detailed. Should she and her little boy be left alone without support in *los Estados Unidos* while her husband is returned to Mexico, "I would just wait for him," she says. "I know he'd be back. It would be so much easier and less risky for him to come back to us than for us to go after him." She laughed in anticipation of her next words. "He may not have any shoes left on his feet, but he'd make it back."

Then lines furrow her face. "Though I've been jesting and laughing, the situation is very serious. We ourselves know, first of all, we're not here on any kind of legal status, and that in itself creates fear. And because we do not speak or read English, we're constantly in fear and don't know if what people tell us is true or not. We live in constant anxiety of what the next day might bring. I might say everything's fine, but that's not true. The worry about being captured is always in the back of our minds." And then a smile parts her lips again. "We take a lot of aspirins."

So why did they cross over into the United States—and remain here—when they are forced to live in such constant dread of the next moment?

"To work," Irma explains simply. "There's very little work in Mexico."

But Elfida's answer is more profound, more to the heart of the matter. "We don't necessarily come here because of the work, but because there's a better way of living here," she says, seriousness filling her dark eyes. "We can provide better for our families."

Sacrifices. Survival at the expense of dignity and education. Only one of the sisters' six children attends school in Midland, because the language barrier instantly would set them apart as *mojados*.

Despite abuses, anxiety and fear, Elfida and Irma say they have every intention of remaining in the United States—and returning again and again if they are sent back to Mexico.

"*Sí,* that can be expected," says Elfida, and grim determination fills her features. "Our belief in this country and desire for it is so great the risks are worth it."

Even if they must hide—and keep on hiding, every day of their lives.

Ricardo surveys a Glasscock County ranch.

An Alien Struggle

※

*H*e's the illegal man.

Some call him alien. Others know him more bluntly as wet-back. And to a few Spanish-speaking individuals, he's *mojado*—wet.

It's easy to forget he's also a person.

In his heart he carries the same fears, hopes, and dreams as any other human being, the same feelings of love, joy, and grief. Yet, faced with the starvation and sheer survival needs of his family, he finds those emotions amplified a hundredfold. They compel him to leave home and loved ones and journey toward the indistinct northern horizon which holds all their fates. Once beyond the Rio Grande, his life becomes one of desperation, his concept of the future a hazy image of his wife and children opening arms wide to receive him back. And his hope, to give them at last the inalienable things which basic human principle says everyone deserves.

His name is Ricardo. Forty-two years old and on his third venture into the United States, he works on a fencing crew with five other illegal immigrants on a sprawling Glasscock County ranch. Back home in San Felipe, Guanajuato, six hundred miles deep in Mexico, he has a wife and six children, ranging in age from toddlers to a twenty-year-old son. Only a few weeks have passed since he last "crossed over," yet he already is beginning to feel twinges of the vast loneliness with which many illegals must cope.

A stocky man in blue jeans and well-worn boots, Ricardo usually works from seven a.m. to six p.m. stretching fence or doing other ranch chores with the help of his fellow laborers and the rancher. Compared to his native Guanajuato, the heat is oppressive here. He guards his skull against the sun with a straw hat, but beads of sweat still glisten on his brow, stream down his neck to form dark splotches about the tiny cross dangling in the V of his partially unbuttoned shirt.

Provided lodging and supplies, Ricardo and his *compadres* spend an hour every evening making tortillas and cooking grub over an open fire in a tin lean-to beside a remote ranch house. And when he closes his eyes to be serenaded to sleep by the gurgle of a nearby windmill and the lowing of cattle, he sees only another hard stretch of work awaiting him on the morrow, and on every succeeding day. Only in his dreams can he ever awaken in the arms of his wife and find his children about him.

Standing this day in brittle-grassed prairie broken only by fence posts marching into depressions and up knolls, Ricardo talks quietly about the country of his birth that he has been forced again to abandon.

To him, the land of his father and grandfather always has been but a valley of the shadow of death: paralyzed, not progressing agriculturally or economically, void of opportunity. Jobs in rural areas, if available at all, are temporary and offer little pay. Work in the cities is more plentiful, but again wages are low, and the typical laborer would rather cross over and pocket the cash tendered by American employers. With seven persons to support, Ricardo had little choice but to do so himself. Back in Guanajuato, he could make only starvation wages doing farm and ranch work—the only job he truly knows. Here, Ricardo's wages are many times that, and with free board he is able to bankroll almost every dollar.

"If I make one hundred fifty dollars, I send one hundred forty home," he says in Spanish, explaining he keeps only enough to buy incidentals such as cigarettes. "Working conditions are just better here. My boss treats me well. Conditions are not good in Mexico. You can get only real little jobs—it just depends where you go there."

When Ricardo left Guanajuato and its dry-land farms, he left a state and people savaged by drought. "Wherever a drought exists in Mexico, that's the region where you'll find more persons crossing over from," he says.

The sky and its clouds are beyond human control and can only be accepted, but the Mexican government is another matter. Ricardo has heard that in parts of his country a person can receive food and acquire federal aid to fund construction of a house, but the details are a blur and hope virtually nil.

"Mexico is a big country," he says without bitterness, "and most of the time you don't receive anything." Only by sharecropping for owners of large ranches might a person gain benefits, he adds.

Six weeks ago Ricardo decided he had little choice but to cross over once more. With three male companions, he traveled by auto from San Felipe to Ciudad Acuña on the banks of the Rio Grande directly across from Del Rio. A few miles outside the sister cities, they crossed the international river in full light of day, though most fellow *mojados* slink across under cover of dark to avoid *la Migra*—the Border Patrol. But night, says Ricardo, brings added dangers: the possibility of slipping in deep water or falling prey to rattlers' fangs, desert thorns, disorientation.

Carrying only the clothes on his back, a couple of snacks, and a small jug of juice, Ricardo now was faced with a vast stretch of arid terrain plagued by drought—a virtual wasteland. It swallowed him and his *compadres*—and Mexico became a memory. Avoiding roadways and towns, Ricardo struggled by foot across backcountry ruled by vulture and *vibora*—the snake—for two long weeks. He survived by gaining handouts at ranch houses, sipping water at windmills. This he had learned from word-of-mouth and experience. Prior to his first venture into America, *mojados* returning to San Felipe had told him where to seek work and which routes to follow. Too, he had come with a man who had crossed over before and knew the ropes.

On that quest and the one after it, Ricardo had trekked all the way to Oklahoma and worked two straight years before going home. But now, on his third trip, home was already far behind him again and he no longer was a man, but a *mojado*. Two of his fellow *mojados* found work at a ranch along the way, but he and the third pushed on, sleeping on the ground, enduring the relentless heat, ignoring the aches and blisters. By the time they reached the Glasscock County ranch to join four men from San Durango on the fencing crew, almost two hundred miles of rugged terrain lay behind them and fifteen days had passed since Ricardo had said "*Vaya con Dios*" to his family in San Felipe.

They had succeeded in eluding *la Migra* this time. In fact, only once in Ricardo's three trips across has the Border Patrol even given him a passing glance. As he unwisely followed a road on that occasion, *la Migra* drove by, looked, and continued on. They must have been going to work or returning from it, he says, to have ignored him so.

Now separated from his wife and children by conditions beyond anyone's control, Ricardo worries about them, and they about him. "They hear a lot of stories about *hombres* drowning trying to cross the river, and of other accidents," he says. But beyond the concern is the realization they will not be together again for a long while—just how long, Ricardo is not sure. He would like to bring his oldest son or entire family over to stay, but to do so would mean they too would have to live every day in fear, not in hope as they do now.

The great dream in Ricardo's life, the one that haunts his nights and rules his days, is to become a citizen of the United States and see his family immigrate legally. Back in Monterrey, Mexico, Ricardo acquired papers he hoped would allow him legal entry, and in Oklahoma he furthered his attempts. But all endeavors have failed thus far, and he remains a *mojado* hunted by the U.S. Border Patrol.

He is a hard worker—"the best hand I've got," says the rancher—but opportunity does not seem to exist in Mexico on the level it does beyond the Rio Grande. And as long as such conditions abide beneath the hot Mexican sun, Ricardo, the "illegal man," will continue his pilgrimages into the United States in search of a better chance in life.

Lariat and Hot Iron

From an airport one mile away comes the blast of jet engines.

But here, on the edge of open country stretching flat and treeless into the north, the present and its technological achievements are a memory, while yesteryear blazes to life in the bellow of cattle, odor of burnt flesh, and heat of iron glowing orange at the design.

It is branding season on Scharbauer Brothers and Company's Crowley Ranch in Midland County, and before the day is over more than one hundred head of Hereford cattle will be rounded up, penned, roped, marked.

The sun rises through white wisps, a swollen mass of fire, and toward it rides the silhouette of a twentieth-century ranch hand outfitted with the essentials of his legendary predecessor, the cowboy: cutting horse, boots, spurs, chaps, jeans, bandana, hat bent like the prow of a ship. No "urban cowboy" here who sips longnecks in some sleazy western bar where the only bull has neither horns nor tail and withers only of metal, for this ranch hand, says co-owner Clarence Scharbauer III, is a real cowpuncher, the kind that can ride and rope instead of drink and pretend. At his flanks on this day ride eleven other men, rounding up cattle, cutting out those which need the brand of the Scharbauer Brothers: a "5" on the left side.

A bull runs astray. Horse and rider whirl in pursuit and, within seconds, slash across its path to halt its stampede. A calf spooks, bolts into the open. Lariat snakes outward, the loop popping taut about its neck. A gate to the pens creaks open and shrill whistles pierce the air as a hundred head of cattle storm within, little dust clouds pluming up from their hooves.

The calves are penned together, and the scrutinizing eyes of a dozen ranch hands check over this year's crop of bulls. Keep one, castrate one. The genes spell the difference.

No wood blaze crackles on this frigid winter day when swirls of dust sweep across boots, yet ribbons of fire nevertheless lap the metal of branding irons. For the twentieth century with its butane has made ever-so-slight inroads even here, and soon the torch-like flames cook the irons to a deep orange.

The present fades into the past as quickly as it surfaced. Astride cutting horse, the ranch hand watches lariat lash outward, slapping against hooves, closing tightly on rear legs, upending the white-face by dragging it halfway across the pen.

It is a bull calf, but its genetic makeup already has determined its fate. Seven ranch hands are hellbent-for-leather toward it, tossing the animal in the air, leaving its left flank skyward. One pins its foreleg between his knees. Another sprawls to slap a boot to the dirt-side groin, grasps rear leg and tail. A third de-ticks the ears. A fourth carves twin incisions in the skull, slashing away the nubs of the horns. A fifth injects a hypodermic needle at the shoulder, vaccinating for blackleg and malignant edema. A sixth rips at the scrotum with a pocket knife, castrating. And the seventh presses blazing iron against flesh, red hair flaming orange.

It is over in seconds, and the calf is up, sprinting away.

Just one of a hundred. Lariat darts outward again like the strike of a rattler.

No glamorous, shoot-'em-up western. Not for this ranch hand. Leave the Indians and the showdowns and oak tree hangings to the spaghetti westerns. This cowpuncher has a job to do. It puts meat in the supermarket, food in the gut. It's the Old West as it really was, springing to life, just for a day.

His work done, the ranch hand leans back in the saddle to the creak of leather. He shifts uneasily at a sudden noise, something a lifetime removed from the lowing of cattle, sizzling of hot iron, popping of lariat.

Glancing skyward he sees a 737 drifting overhead, bound for a twentieth-century rendezvous with a prairieland runway a Winchester shot away.

The Last Cowboy

*T*hey say legends die hard—legends of men facing overwhelming odds, of the antihero who gains the admiration of friend and foe alike, of the lone man who raises a fist to the sky and challenges the entire world, and wins.

Such is the saga of Charles Ray "Cowboy" Walls, whose incredible eleven-day odyssey in 1976 carried him from the slashing and timeless Coke County canyons to his destiny beside two shining rails halfway across the continent. An episode testifying to the eternal quests of all men without peace, it forever branded him into the lore and legend of the Pecos country.

He was considered by some to be a nineteenth-century man trying to cope with a twentieth-century world, an imposing figure at six feet seven and 270 to 290 pounds who had been born out of time and yearned for the rugged, two-fisted life the Old West had offered.

Dreams. Reality. Seldom do they become one. They didn't in thirty-one years for Charlie, and finally—spurred by reasons only he ever would know—he made his play, by plan or impulse, and created his *own* world.

It would disintegrate within a fortnight, but not before he had ridden hellbent-for-leather through it and, perhaps, ultimately found true peace.

Born the youngest of nine children June 13, 1944, in Blackwell, Texas, he grew up on ranches amid the gullies, buttes, and cedar brakes of the Colorado River watershed in Coke County, a brown-haired, green-eyed boy advancing toward manhood and, say some, finding himself increasingly ill at ease in a technological age.

"He was a guy that was probably born about a hundred and fifty years too late," said Marshall Millican, who first knew Charlie in the late 1960s when Charlie and Millican's father both worked on the same ranch. "He was kind of a cowboy. . . . He would liked to have lived . . . way back when, I think. That was just my impression of him [because of] the way he did, just the kind of guy he was."

"He enjoyed horses and the Old West type of life," noted J. Lee Ensor, Coke County sheriff from 1974 to 1981 and an acquaintance of Charlie's.

"He was a man that lived about forty or fifty years [in the past], way back in the teens or twenties" despite it actually being the sixties and seventies, said longtime Texas Ranger Arthur Sikes, who also knew him from a lawman's standpoint.

Charlie's yearning for the Old West may have taken root in his boyhood, when Wayne McCabe came to know him; Charlie, in the 1950s, lived on a Silver-area ranch owned by McCabe's brother, who employed Charlie's father. "Charlie liked good horses . . . and had the idea he'd liked to have lived a hundred years ago," noted McCabe, who conceded that he never heard Charlie voice the notion in so many words.

Indeed, Charlie's sisters, Helen Mathers and Joy Spradlin, stopped short of corroborating the statement. "I can't say that for sure," reflected Mrs. Mathers. "I don't think anybody could—except him. I've heard that myself; I've heard people say that. Maybe he talked to them more than he did me. But I'm his sister and I never heard him say it. He lived a western life, if that's where it's coming from. *I* like the Old West; does that make *me* a strange person?"

"I know he loved the country [and] he loved horses," said Mrs. Spradlin, Charlie's senior by five years. "But I don't see anything strange about that. He was just a normal, average kid growing up. He wasn't someone that would stand out."

Nevertheless, the perception of many of those who knew Charlie as an adult was that his demeanor, his dress, his pursuits bespoke a man living an Old West fantasy in a New West reality. As he grew to towering maturity he often veiled his face behind a full beard like an old-time trail driver. He seldom was without cowboy hat and western shirt, and townspeople on city sidewalks needed only hear the rasp of his jeans or click of his boots to know he was approaching. If any doubt remained, one glance at his feet settled the matter: Charlie always split his boots, front and back, and laced them. On his shoulders he carried descriptive tattoos: "Goat Roper" and "Texas." While many persons called him "Charlie" (the only name by which his family knew him), he allowed some to address him more descriptively as "Roper," and still others came to know him as "Cowboy."

It all seemed an outgrowth of a basic personality hewn by a fascination for the quintessential cowboy of the Old West—a simpler, more caring era when men spoke only when they had something to say and when no passing stranger rode away hungry from anyone's door. Indeed, Charlie was quiet to the point of making "John Wayne look like a blabber-mouth," noted Roy Ivey, an acquaintance. "He never had much to say. . . . He's definitely a loner."

"He didn't put out a special effort to be with people," amplified Mrs. Spradlin, who seldom saw him after he reached adulthood. "He was with [our] mother a lot and he loved his kids. [But] about him being a loner, he really was. He *liked* to be alone. [But] he enjoyed people when he was with them."

And many persons found him basically a good man.

"Everybody said Charlie was a good-hearted fellow," said Ensor. "He was very likable."

Ernest Haynes, who knew Charlie strictly from the standpoint of Haynes's mid-1970s position as chief deputy of Tom Green County Sheriff's Department, put it in typical West Texas terms: "He was an easy-going ol' boy."

Even though it was hard to live a cowboy's life in the modern world.

Charlie Walls at age sixteen in Grand Prairie High School. (Courtesy Joy Spradlin)

He attended high school in Grand Prairie, dropped out at midterm his senior year, and then served a hitch in the Navy, an experience that may have left a cowboy only chomping at the bit like a wild mustang. He tried his spurs at rodeoing, an artificial cowboying world still a century removed from the real one. Distant too were the days of riding drift fences in roundups and pushing herds up the trail; Charlie could get no closer than working as a ranch hand and driving a cattle truck—and even then he seemed miscast to some.

"Charlie wasn't much of a hand, really," said Marshall Millican, recalling the days Charlie worked with Millican's father on the Bill and Marvin Simpson ranch in Coke County. "He'd ride [horseback] . . . [and] liked to call himself a cowboy. But in my

The Last Cowboy

opinion, Charlie *wasn't* a cowboy. . . . He was somebody that would have *liked* to have been."

Maybe all he needed was a chance—but like the horses which acquaintance Melvin Childress said Charlie knew "real well," true old-time cowboys just didn't have a place any more in a ranching industry ruled by pickups, cattle trucks, and "roundup" motorcycles and helicopters.

Charlie went through an unsuccessful marriage that brought him four children, and somewhere along the line began to drink on occasion. Whether it all stemmed from disillusionment with the modern world, only he ever would know—just as only he would know what role disenchantment played in his eventual tangles with the law.

His troubles all began in the late 1960s after he left the employ of the Simpson brothers. Later-lawman Marshall Millican, who was a sophomore in high school at the time, was an eyewitness to the incident:

> Charlie and a friend of his came out there [to the Simpson Ranch in Coke County] and tried to steal some saddles out of the barn. And my dad [Elton Millican] confronted them . . . [with] a shotgun that didn't have any shells in it . . . and made them put it back. . . . I came in about that time and I had the twenty-two rifle down there at the barn—it was laying up there in the corner—and I sneaked around and got it and gave it to Daddy. And Charlie, at one point in time, run in and grabbed the gun from Daddy. They fought and scuffled with it. And finally Charlie broke and ran off.

It was the lone documented act of violence ever on Charlie's part, despite the allegation of a later fellow jail inmate [who requested anonymity] that, although he normally was unemotional, "when he has problems, whenever he's drinking, he can be very violent."

Even when Melvin Childress, sheriff of Coke County, arrested Charlie in the saddle incident, he offered "no resistance," said Childress. "He never seemed to be a violent-type man."

"They had a pretty good round over those saddles that night," said later-sheriff Ensor, "but that's really about the only physical thing I know of on Charlie. . . . As far as harming anybody or things like that, he wasn't an aggressor."

Indicted January 15, 1968, for burglary, Charlie was sentenced in Fifty-first District Court February 5, 1968, to three years in the state penitentiary, a sentence which the court probated. Although he never served time for the incident, more difficulties with the law ensued. Perhaps it was inevitable for a man both free and bound, a cowboy possibly trapped by his own nineteenth-century personality. On February 11, 1975, Charlie stole a jeep valued at one thousand dollars, tools, and a saddle from the Raymond Taylor holdings about ten miles south of Tennyson. In that same month, he also took a saddle, two lariats, a saddle blanket, three headstalls, an extension cord, and tools from the Dean Eubanks stock farm near Blackwell. Driving northward in the jeep February 25, he pawned a portion of the tack items and tools in Abilene and the remainder in Wichita Falls. As he reached Shawnee, Oklahoma, the following day, law officers either recognized the jeep as stolen or sought to stop him on a traffic violation. In the high-speed chase which ensued, he tried to ensure his getaway by gunning the open-topped vehicle through a barbed wire fence; the top strand peeled him right off.

Life for a cowboy-out-of-time always seemed that way.

Returned for incarceration in Tom Green County Jail and indicted March 6 for theft over two hundred dollars, this man who so cherished solitude and open country exhibited understandable moodiness while awaiting trial. After each visit by Charlie's girlfriend, according to the unnamed fellow inmate, Charlie would just "isolate himself from everybody" for hours.

Waiving jury trial and confessing to the third-degree felony in Fifty-first District Court July 11, 1975, Charlie was assessed four years in the state penitentiary. A mustang captured but not broken, he arrived at the state penitentiary at Huntsville August 14, 1975, and endured seven months as an apparently model prisoner to gain parole March 19, 1976. Terms of his release included the provision that he report regularly to his parole officer.

For this maverick man, it evidently was too much to ask.

In mid-May 1976, Charlie drifted down to Sabinal in the Hill Country and, for one last time, perhaps, sought in the green-splashed canyonlands to make peace with the modern era. The idyllic setting and companionship of longtime friends Mr. and Mrs. Walter Douglas Cook and their five children soothed but did not heal; the apparent turmoil surged inexorably toward a climax that soon would hurl him headlong into an unparalleled adventure.

"To me and my family, he was not an outlaw or a bandit," recalled Mrs. Cook, who met Charlie in San Angelo in about 1966 and knew him as "Roper."

> He was grateful for every bite we fed him, and we went swimming, drove around in the hills, and he even caught a bull snake and my oldest son made a pet of it. I gave Charlie two pairs of pants and three or four shirts and a pair of black cowboy boots [that he] . . . split in front and back as he said he never wore a pair of boots that he didn't cut. . . . He was really proud to get those because the ones he had, which weren't cowboy boots, were nearly worn out, and he had cut the back side out because his heels were so sore from walking.
>
> I had no idea that Charlie was in trouble as he didn't talk much as everyone knew. . . . When he left Sabinal, on the road, he said, "Someday soon, when I decide to settle down, I'm coming back to Utopia to spend the rest of my life." Utopia is a little town just north of Sabinal in the hills.

But Charlie's Utopia awaited elsewhere, in another form: He would spend the rest of his life being the cowboy that he perhaps always should have been.

Whether it was one individual event which finally spurred him into raising his fist to the twentieth century or the culmination of three decades, no one ever will know. But by plan or oversight, Charlie shunned his parole officer, thereby forfeiting his brief respite from the "crossbar hotel." Too, law officers discovered his fingerprints at a burglarized cabin on E. V. Spence Reservoir near Robert Lee, and suspected him in other burglaries along a line from Spence to Oak Creek Lake near Blackwell. The break-ins, noted then-Texas Ranger Arthur Sikes, were not with the intent to profit from selling the merchandise; the only motive seemed to be to gain food. "About all he ever done was burglarize . . . hunting cabins to get something to eat, then he'd drink their liquor," he recalled.

"When I went to the first cabins that had been burglarized," recalled J. Lee Ensor, who was sheriff of Coke County by then, "I thought he was . . . still in the penitentiary. And when I walked in, my first remark was, it looked like Charlie."

Then, as day broke bright and warm Tuesday, June 1, 1976, law officials readied a warrant for his arrest.

Excepting the possibility of coincidence, Charlie either learned of it somehow, or saw it coming. For immediately all the pent-up frustration and desires of a cowboy out-of-time finally bolted free once and for all.

It began when someone took a tractor from farmland in southern Coke County and—as shown by the tracks—bowled over fences in bearing northward through fields and pastures until the machine bogged in the mud. Sikes later theorized it was Charlie, traveling cross-country into increasingly rugged canyonland.

Between five p.m. and dusk on Wednesday, June 2, a Mexican ranch hand at an isolated line camp on the Wayne McCabe Ranch, approximately sixteen miles southwest of Robert Lee and three miles east of Highway 2034, looked up to see a towering man with full beard approaching a step at a time. Here on the Divide, at the brink of gaping Colorado River watershed canyons with battlements of limestone and virtually impenetrable cedars, to see a stranger on foot was unusual, evoking bewilderment. The ranch hand observed that, in addition to a transistor radio, the man carried a twenty-two caliber rifle. Too, he noted the bandana about his neck and the odd footwear—cowboy boots split down the front and laced. The worker believed him only a neighbor stranded by vehicle trouble, so he did not resist when the big stranger took a horse and saddle, jug of water, food, twenty-two caliber cartridges, and eight packs of cigarettes.

"He never . . . pulled a gun on him; he just took the horse and saddled him," recalled Wayne McCabe, who gained his information from the ranch hand. "The horse was a registered quarter horse. A sorrel gelding, he was a good cow horse [then fifteen years old] which I rode for twenty years. . . . The ranch hand felt sure he was a neighbor wanting to borrow the horse for some purpose, a neighbor . . . that needed to get home."

Wherever "home" was, the hand knew it had to lie to the west, for he watched the stranger mount up and literally ride off into the sunset.

"As [he] rode off," Wayne McCabe related, "he pulled a bandana up across his nose and mouth and said, '*Adios, amigo.*' The Mexican hand, Pedro, knew then his horse was being stolen."

To the uninitiated, it seemed without purpose or motivation, an incident cloaked in mystery. "He sure picked a strange thing to do," a Texas Highway Patrol trooper soon would be philosophizing. "He can go rob a bank and go to the penitentiary ten years, but he decides to do this and go to the penitentiary ten years." But when the ranch hand went for help—four miles away— and told his story, those who knew Charles Ray "Cowboy" Walls understood.

"This is his 'thing,'" reflected one ranch owner as he stood surveying the rugged cedar land which had swallowed the rider. "All his life he's always said he was born too late, that he should've lived a hundred years ago."

And when Charlie—if indeed it were he—spurred the gelding westward down a lane and onto Highway 2034, then through a north-side gate into the Fred McCabe Ranch and made for the canyons, he disappeared forever into the frontier of which he perhaps always should have been a part.

By nightfall a dragnet was under way, pitting modern-day technology against the instincts of a cowboy on a good horse. First on the scene were Coke County Sheriff J. Lee Ensor and his deputy, Marshall Millican, both of whom considered Charlie immediately. "The physical description fits him and what he's doing fits him," Ensor thought aloud. Too, came Tom Green County chief deputy Ernest Haynes, who noted that "this is the way he [Charlie] operates."

Quickly joining the operation were as many as thirty law officers, representing not only Coke County and Tom Green County sheriff's departments, but the Texas Rangers, Texas Highway Patrol,

The Fred McCabe pasture gate through which Charlie Walls disappeared into a New West frontier.

Sterling County Sheriff's Department, and Texas Parks and Wildlife Department. With darkness blanketing the Divide and canyons, Sheriff Ensor could only set up roadblocks along highways 2034 and 158, arrange to bring in horses and a Midland Department of Public Safety helicopter, and wait for daybreak.

Meanwhile, the cowboy picked his way down gutting canyons, through dense underbrush, across tableland. It was a virtual wilderness through which he rode, a savage land of inverted mountains where the flats of the Divide ran out over the breaks of the Colorado River watershed like bony and broken fingers. The high country at 2,500 feet held open grassland interspersed with mesquites, scrub cedars, and prickly pear, but at sentineling rimrock it suddenly plunged four hundred feet to canyon bottoms jungled with briars and great spidery cedars and choked by boulders, drift dams, and deadfall. It encompassed tens of thousands of acres within a great "V" formed by highways 2034 and 158, and never before had it so yielded to an unfenced maverick.

"[The country] was terribly rough," remembered Ensor. "You could get down in those canyons and you could walk there for a good long ways at a time and not even . . . [have] the sun hit you."

Sunrise Thursday likely found Charlie crouched in the cedars alongside his horse as the animal shifted uneasily to the whir of a chopper in the sky. The dawning also found a modern-day posse mounting horses back at the gate along Highway 2034, with the rays glinting from semiautomatic weapons and hand-held communications devices. And even as the manhunt commenced, lawmen acquainted with Charlie knew just what they were up against.

"Charlie was a fellow you couldn't out-think, because he kind of had a pattern all of his own," noted Ensor.

"Cowboy Walls," reflected lead investigator and Texas Ranger Arthur Sikes, "was the kind of person that [was] like a coyote: he could travel in the dark in strange country better than I could in the daytime. Of course, he *knew* that country, and he could travel it in the dark very, very well."

"He was raised . . . in the ranching country and he knew how to get around in it, where[as] most people wouldn't," added Wayne McCabe. "He [probably] kind of had an idea where he was going and what he was going to do."

As the chopper bearing Sikes whirred overhead and Ernest Haynes and a fellow Tom Green County deputy scouted the range land by vehicle and foot, the posse entered the backcountry on horseback. There were a half-dozen in the party: a single peace officer (Marshall Millican), and the others just ordinary ranchers and stock farmers—none of whom had been deputized though all but one or two carried firearms. As they began trying to track the cowboy, they, too, quickly realized the formidable foe they faced.

"He went through a gate from the highway, closed it, and by the time he was three horse-lengths from it he had the horse in a gallop," landowner Fred McCabe, Sr. read in the tracks. "He went due north, following a fence row as far as he could go and then headed east when he got to the edge of the canyon. You could see in two or three places where he tried to go down before he finally did. I've been riding this countryside for seventy-four years and I know how hard it is to cross that canyon. You need a devil of a good horse and daylight to do it. I'm sure he crossed it in daylight. When he got to the bottom he headed due west. . . . He back-tracked and see-sawed to beat the dickens, just like somebody would do trying to hide his trail."

"We rode in the pasture and split up in pairs," remembered James Allen, who supplied three of the horses. "Millican had a pistol but I didn't even have a gun. I rode with him; I figured he'd protect me. And we searched several canyons and got on top, and we saw part of his trail where his horse had dropped a deposit. And we tracked him for a ways but then we lost the trail." That point, said Fred McCabe, lay one and a half miles from the gate.

Although later in the day the latter man indicated he intended to sleep with his six-shooter under his pillow, as "sixty, seventy years ago they hung horse thieves from the nearest tree," most of the pursuers who knew Charlie personally, or had been told of him, held little concern for their own welfare.

"We weren't really concerned about him being dangerous at that time," said Allen.

Added Wayne McCabe, a fellow posse member, "We were just mainly looking for the horse."

Even Sheriff Ensor, who had initiated the manhunt, was not overly worried. "We had to take precautions," he explained, "because we knew he had the gun [presumed to be from a burglarized cabin]. Personally, myself, I didn't really consider him as really a dangerous person."

Marshall Millican, whose view of Charlie had been shaped by the long-ago scuffle involving Charlie and his father, alone believed differently. "He was running from the law and he was considered . . . armed and dangerous," said Millican, who was to succeed Ensor as Coke County sheriff in 1981. "I figured probably that he knew he was probably going back to the penitentiary, and had he been confronted I believe . . . he'd've hurt someone. Just lucky that . . . somebody didn't ride up on him whenever he was under one of those cedar bushes out there, because he'd've probably shot somebody."

All that day the posse combed the rugged pasture without sighting the lone horseman, while the helicopter, patrol units, and officers afoot carried the fruitless search far beyond its fences and to every area shack. The sun baked skulls and sent rivulets streaming down faces. Thirst reigned and enthusiasm waned. And the crackle of radios between posse and helicopter and patrol units carried but one communique: The cowboy and his horse had blended with the backcountry as though they always had been a part of it.

Finally, Sheriff Ensor, scouring primitive ranch roads on Divide range land west of that Fred McCabe pasture, slowed his vehicle to study a double line of U-shaped impressions in the ground.

"I started finding his horse tracks where he rode out of that pasture that he rode in to that [first] night, heading west," recalled

Ensor. "Most of the horse tracks were on top, going right down those pasture roads. It was nearly impossible [to find tracks] down in those canyons. . . . The ones that rode that [Fred McCabe] pasture didn't find where he rode out."

Indeed, the horsemen found no evidence that Charlie ever had cut any barbed-and-net-wire fences in riding from pasture to pasture. With some fences in that area "old" and in "pretty bad" shape, said nearby landowner Paul Burns, Charlie likely—as deputy Millican theorized—"stomped the wires down" and crossed his horse.

The opinion of Burns, Wayne McCabe, and Fred McCabe—on whose ranches the search centered—was that Charlie now was lying up in the rocky, forested canyons and would move out across the wilderness when night fell. "There's a few tanks and windmills to water up at, if he can find 'em," Fred McCabe noted at the time. "And he took food and a jug, so he probably won't come out till he wants to."

But Charlie, his lifelong dream perhaps finally in his grasp and the twentieth century trodden under the hooves of his horse, evidently had no intention of yielding his new-found supremacy. Night fell again, and still he rode free, chasing the starry horizon, maybe tasting real life for the first time. Then the eastern sky dawned fiery and orange Friday, and Sheriff Ensor, continuing to comb primitive ranch roads, found more horse tracks.

"He just went nearly in a straight line through pasture gates [which he closed behind him], going west till he got to a pasture," he said.

Authorities, tightening the screws, immediately focused all attention to the west on that rugged pasture, which lay on the Ray Stewart Ranch north of Divide Cemetery. Whereas in the old days the axiom had been "One riot, one ranger," now *four* Texas Rangers chased the cowboy.

Under a huge cedar deep in a green-splashed canyon, Charlie, meanwhile, had unsaddled his horse and taken refuge against the chopper which, for two days, made repeated passes overhead.

"I know the day before [on Thursday], that I was in one when we flew right over that cedar," said Ensor. "I'm sure he or the saddle . . . was under there that time we flew over it."

"I flew over that from four different directions and I couldn't see [anything]," noted then-Texas Ranger Sikes. "But to show you how caring he was, he had unsaddled the horse and laid the saddle down, covered it up with a saddle blanket, and tied the horse in under a big heavy tree where he couldn't be seen from the air."

"[It] looked like he stayed most of the day there [at that] big cedar in the bottom of one of those deep canyons," noted Wayne McCabe, who later studied the site.

At some point Charlie must have realized that even a cowboy sometimes has to leave his horse behind. In his case, it was a matter of remaining horseback and being sighted—and returned to prison—or attacking the backcountry on foot and still having true freedom. So, untying the animal, he let it wander off unencumbered toward the modern world. Then, lifting rifle, food, and jug, Charlie turned to seek his own destiny.

At noon Friday, Texas Ranger Sikes and rancher Wayne McCabe, studying the wilderness from the vantage point of the helicopter, sighted the horse running loose in the highcountry of the Ray Stewart pasture. Arranging for it to be picked up, Sikes returned McCabe to his horse trailer, and again a horseback posse quickly formed where pasture roads gave way to impassable terrain. In this party were deputy Millican, Wayne McCabe, and Burns. As they picked up tracks of the horse and began trailing them where Charlie had pushed hard across the flats in making for a gaping canyon, Burns in particular had reason to appreciate the cowboy's ability to take his horse successfully through such rough country.

"I crippled my horse up there," Burns recalled, "and the DPS helicopter came down and picked me up and took me back to my pickup. . . . I got my trailer and went back up on the Divide and got my horse."

Meanwhile, Millican and McCabe pushed on.

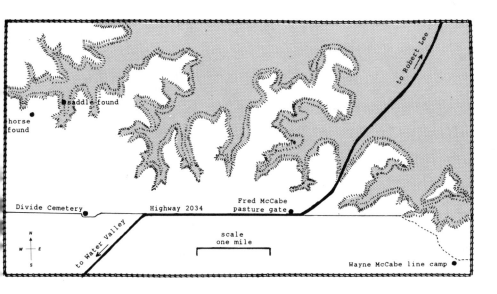

Map of the manhunt area.

"[We] found where he'd rode him off down in one of those ol' deep cedar canyons," recalled Millican, "and then got to tracking him down through there and found . . . where he'd taken the saddle off the horse and throwed it up under a cedar."

Lawmen realized immediately that the cowboy had chosen the site with care.

"All he had to do," noted Ensor, "was sit under that cedar tree when we was flying over hunting him. Because we got *back* in the helicopter after we found the saddle and flew over low, *knowing* they were there, and then we *still* couldn't see them."

The site lay four and one-quarter air miles northwest of the Fred McCabe pasture gate through which Charlie had taken the horse two days before, and almost eight air miles northwest of the Wayne McCabe line camp. Although no one ever would know the exact details of the cowboy's route or how long he might have lain up in intervening canyons, Ensor believed it possible Charlie could have reached the Stewart pasture that first night to plunge the horse down into the deep gulch.

"That wouldn't have been any travel at all for a horse, and he knew the country well," said Ensor.

It was five p.m. when Millican and McCabe discovered the saddle. Four hours of daylight remained, and now they seemed to be closing in; a man on foot seemingly could not get far in daylight in such rugged country with the technology of the 1970s breathing down his neck. But combing the rocky and tangled canyon floor at the site, the two men could find no boot tracks leading away from the saddle.

Then night fell Friday—and the cowboy got away.

"At night—he knew the country—he could travel wherever he wanted to without any problem," noted Ensor.

Incredibly, a man considered by some to be a throwback to the 1800s had defied the officers and equipment of the state's foremost law agencies and escaped somehow to earn the right to notch his gun.

"It's always been a mystery to me," posse member Burns would note years later.

"We're still looking, more or less making a few of these cabins left unattended, but we're gonna have to wait for him now," lamented deputy Millican on the afternoon of Saturday, June 5, after authorities had lifted the dragnet. And when the last posse member loaded his horse back into a pickup trailer and drove away, the legend of "Cowboy" Walls became assured in the annals of the Pecos country.

In reflecting upon the entire episode from the vantage point of fifteen years, some dragnet participants still wondered what *really* motivated Charlie to take that horse and ride off into those canyons. Ensor considered it all a "strange" chapter, while Millican and Wayne McCabe believed Charlie may have only been thinking practically.

"He didn't have anywhere *else* to go," said Millican. "He was just going here, there, and yonder, just living day by day."

Said McCabe, "He was just probably leaving this area . . . and he decided he'd just ride the horse awhile instead of walk."

But to posse member James Allen, something much more complex was at play in Charlie's mind: "I imagine he was a dreamer."

For Charlie, however, it was a dream—and mystery—that only was beginning, though no one would ever tell the tale. A nonpareil odyssey, it had only a genesis and an end, with no middle except for conjecture:

Northward approximately forty miles, the twin rails of Missouri Pacific Railroad stretched east-west across the state, from Fort Worth to Midland to El Paso, and beyond as the Texas and Pacific. Although Texas Ranger Sikes and Deputy Millican theorized Charlie hitched a ride on a westbound truck near Sterling City, the cowboy may have considered it too risky for the object of a massive manhunt to face passing motorists openly. Instead, in the Colorado City area, he may have hopped a fast freight to the horizon like Depression-era hoboes, thus again achieving oneness with the past.

If so, he probably had no destination, neither east nor west, but the first freight which thundered by could have been a westbounder ready for the grabbing. As diesel smoke from the locomotive drifted back down the line of cars and the wheels roared, the train may have carried him inexorably toward the setting sun, through the Trans-Pecos crags, the southern New Mexico badlands, the Arizona deserts. Whom he met on the rails—if indeed he were there—what incidents befell him, which emotions carried him onward to the clickety-click of wheels across rail joints, no one can say. But as Sunday, June 13, neared an end, one thing is certain: Charlie had reached the West Coast—San Bernardino, California, to be exact.

It was the cowboy's thirty-second birthday. It would be his last. He bought a bottle of booze or perhaps shared one in a hobo jungle. He drank. Maybe he reflected on his life, the past eleven days, sensed identification with the renegade cowboy fighting the encroachment of civilization in *Lonely Are the Brave*. Perhaps, even, he made peace with himself.

Dusk found him in an area of the freight yards frequented by tramps. Here, two sets of rails stretched north and south, leading only into the future, not the past. Maybe he planned. Maybe he despaired. Maybe, even, he fought. Only he ever would know. Positioning himself between the two tracks, he waited.

A freight train barreled through at 9:35 p.m. At 10:20, engineer J. W. Hackfield of an approaching Amtrak train noticed a form on the ground delineated by the headlight of the locomotive. Halting, the train crew discovered a man's body, the leg severed by the wheels of a freight and the boots strangely split and laced.

Several days later, Sheriff Ensor and Texas Ranger Sikes each received phone calls from San Bernardino authorities; Sikes had issued an all-points bulletin on Charlie during the manhunt.

"California said, 'We believe we might have your man—he's dead, killed by a freight train,'" recalled Sikes. "I said 'Did they tell you what tattoos he had? His girlfriend told me thirteen tattoos.' And they said, 'That's him.'"

Thus, quickly and tragically, in the dusk of busy freight yards a thousand miles away from the wilderness canyons of Coke County, ended the life of Charles Ray Walls, perhaps the last real cowboy.

Investigating his death, Sikes made seventeen phone calls to various San Bernardino authorities. He learned, among other details, that the coroner's office considered it merely an accident.

Charlie, ruled San Bernardino deputy coroner Gene Dupertuis, had "definitely been drinking" and "evidently just walked into the side of a moving train. There's nothing more to tell."

No one walks into the side of a moving train.

He may commit suicide by walking in *front* of a train, he may die accidentally trying to *catch* a train, or someone may knock him in the head and throw him *off* or *under* a train.

But no one just walks into the side of a moving train.

More than fifteen years after Charlie's death, former West Texas lawmen remained dissatisfied not only with the coroner's conclusion, but with the San Bernardino law officers' investigation of the matter.

"There never was a, what I could see, a great investigation," reflected Ensor, who left law enforcement in 1981. "It was my understanding [there were] quite a few witnesses there. The report back to Texas was very vague. . . . There really wasn't anything, you might say, black-and-white."

Texas's lead investigator Sikes, long-retired from the Rangers in 1991, reflected on those enigmatic events in the San Bernardino freight yards and remained convinced Charlie's death was far from accidental.

> I think he was murdered. His pocketknife was out [and] open and it was lying close to his body. . . . He had been hit in the back by the steps on a boxcar, [but] all information leads me to believe that he was pushed into the train. . . . It was down in a part where hoboes would stay, cooking in tin cans, [a] hobo jungle. . . . The knife was identified as Walls's as it and his boots were sent back [to Texas] with his body. . . . He was definitely killed by a train [but] I think it was homicide. But I couldn't prove that.

The family, too, never accepted the coroner's conclusion. "My husband and my twin brother went to the funeral home [when the body was returned for burial near Blackwell] to identify him," said Charlie's sister Joy Spradlin, who added that they identified the body on the basis of known scars from a horse bite and an automobile accident. "[There had been] a blow to the back of his head and . . . the leg severed, and you don't walk into a train and come out like that—you won't have a face left, and it won't do the damage on the *back* of your head. He was also robbed; he had no billfold. He never went without his billfold.

"I think he was murdered. He's dead, and probably to [some] that wouldn't matter; he's gone. But it *does* matter; it matters to us."

And so in death, the cowboy continued to be as mysterious as in life.

What really happened that night beside those rails in California? What truly befell Charlie in the ensuing eleven days after he took the horse? And, most important, perhaps, did he ever truly find a cowboy's peace in a world that had no place for one?

The answers lie hidden deep in the legends of the Pecos frontier.

Reflecting on Charlie's life and death, lawmen, family, and friends reached far into the cowboy's heart and found a man whom the world perhaps never understood.

"He wasn't 'bad,'" said former Texas Ranger Sikes.

"He wasn't what you'd call a bad guy at all," amplified Wayne McCabe. "He was a pretty good fellow, in a way. He was really just more harm to himself than anybody else."

"Charlie was a harmless fellow," said former Coke County Sheriff Ensor. "Nobody really condemned Charlie . . . as being a cruel man or a really rough person or anything like that. He just had some ways that didn't work."

"I don't want to paint him as a lily white, because he wasn't," said his sister Joy Spradlin. "He just got off on the wrong track. There's a lot of people that do that. I know he wasn't the best person in the world, but he wasn't the worst."

"I know he did things he shouldn't have," agreed another sister, Helen Mathers. "I'm the first one to admit that. But I know he was a good-hearted man."

The most moving epitaph of all came from longtime friend Mrs. Walter Douglas Cook of Sabinal:

> In this modern day and time I can hardly believe that "Cowboy" Walls was one to be so careless as to get killed in the muddle of a city in California. I believe that Charlie, having served in the Navy, actually served his country and served society. As I understand, he was a very good prisoner, else he wouldn't have gotten out so soon. . . . In Charlie's own mind, he may have blocked

out the city sidewalks and everything of modern-day times. He could have stolen a Cadillac or taken over a train, but instead he chose a horse. At least he murdered no man, and who is to be Charlie's judge?

I liked the guy for what he was inside, not for what he had done. May God rest his soul, because I do believe God has a place for cowboys, even 'cowboys' like Charlie. He didn't die at daybreak, at least he got to see a last sunset. I uphold no criminal, but in a way I'm glad he wasn't caught, because the next time he would have been like a wild stallion.

Ride on, Charlie, through that peaceful, free land beyond the sky.

The Last Cowboy

Notes on Sources

⚛

The Lost Chisos Mine

For background history on Presidio de San Vicente, I am indebted to Ronnie C. Tyler, *The Big Bend: A History of the Last Texas Frontier* (Washington: National Park Service, 1975), 19, 30, 31, 42, 43, 44-45, 48-49, 54-55, 90-91, 135, 136, 138, 257-58, 262; Carlysle Graham Raht, *The Romance of Davis Mountains and Big Bend Country* (Odessa: The Rahtbooks Company, Edition Texana, 1963), 45, 46, 333, 373, 374; and Max L. Moorhead, *The Presidio: Bastion of the Spanish Borderlands* (Norman: University of Oklahoma Press, first paperback printing 1991), 166. The quote regarding Zapato Tuerto, information regarding the word "Chisos," and the report of La Llorona in the old mission vicinity are as recounted by Elton Miles, *Tales of the Big Bend* (College Station: Texas A&M Press, 1976), 36, 39, 40, 41, 44.

Quotations from Robert T. Hill are from his "Running the Cañons of the Rio Grande," a transcript of which is in my possession. The quotes attributed to T. W. Chandler are from William H. Emory, *Report on the United States and Mexican Boundary Survey, Vol. 1* (Austin: Texas State Historical Association, 1987), 83, 84. I drew upon Ross A. Maxwell, *Big Bend Country* (Big Bend National Park: Big Bend Natural History Association, 1985), 5, 12, 15, 28, 30-32, for background on area mines and accounts of alleged finds.

The directional clue said to be gained on the thirteenth or seventeenth of May is from Victor J. Smith, "Lost Mines of the Chisos Mountains" (*Sul Ross State Teachers College Bulletin #1*, December 1926).

Information on the speleological survey of Mt. Emory Cave is from Dale L. Pate, compiler, "The Deep Caves of Texas," *The Texas Caver*, December 1990, 127. Mt. Emory Cave is listed as the twenty-sixth deepest cave in Texas.

I conducted pertinent interviews with Simon Bernal, Midland, Texas, 1983 and 15 March 1991; James Owens, Midland, 1983, 1989, and 10 March 1990; Thomas B. Henderson, Marathon, Texas, 9 February 1990; and Francis Rooney, by telephone to Marathon, 14 October 1990. Family members of Juan Gamboa conducted an interview with Gamboa at my request, Midland, 1983.

In 1989 Richard Galle of Midland passed along the story of the reported "ghost bells" of the old mission. Galle gained the account from one of the two witnesses.

I also drew upon my personal investigation of the Chisos backcountry.

Phantoms and Ghost Lights

For background on the legend of La Llorona, I relied upon *More Tales of the Big Bend* by Elton Miles (College Station, Texas A&M Press, 1988), 37; and my interview with Joe Primera, Fort Stockton, Texas, 7 April 1983.

I conducted pertinent interviews with James Owens, Midland, Texas, 1983; Lee Harris, Fort Stockton, winter 1983; Rose Duarte, Fort Stockton, 23 February 1983; Gloria Dupre, Fort Stockton, 23 February 1983; Thomas B. Henderson, Marathon, Texas, 9 February 1990; W. R. Green, Marathon, 9 February 1990; Lou Ashmore and Alice Ashmore, Midland, spring 1985; Lee Ann Ballew, by telephone to Andrews, Texas, 25 May 1991; Ortha Huff, by telephone to San Angelo, Texas, spring 1976; and my grandmother, Lucy B. Dearen, Sterling City, Texas, 12 December 1976 and 11 November 1982.

Robert Ellison's account of his 1883 sighting of mysterious lights and the quote attributed to him are from Marge Crumbaker, "The Unsolved Mystery of the Ghost Light" (*Texas Tempo Magazine*, a supplement to the *Houston Post*, 7 January 1968).

Dr. John Desmond's quote is from Hallie Stillwell, "Ghost Lights Seen Through Years in Mountains of Big Bend County" (*The Times Sunday Magazine*), undated clipping in my possession.

The account of the headless horseman at Shafter Lake is from a television interview with Virginia Irwin, circa 1983.

Information regarding Shafter's expedition is from John Howard Griffin, *Land of the High Sky* (Midland: The First National Bank of Midland, 1959), 61; and Shafter's report, as contained in "Shafter's Explorations in Western Texas, 1875," *West Texas Historical Association Year Book Vol. 9*, October 1933, 82-96.

The Davis Mountains Spirit

This account is based primarily on interviews I taped 26 June 1983 with Karen and Forrest Keefe during their occupancy of the house in Jeff Davis County, Texas, and on my personal investigation of the site, 26-27 June 1983.

Other pertinent interviews I conducted were with Jim Hayman, Fort Stockton, Texas, 7 April 1983, and by telephone to Jeff Davis County, summer 1983; John Ryan, by telephone to Jeff Davis County, summer 1983; Rod Crowder, by telephone to Fort Davis, Texas, summer 1983; and Dorothy Nigrelli, by telephone to Jeff Davis County, summer 1983.

Big Bend Ranch

This chapter is based partly on my exploration of Big Bend Ranch by foot, four-wheel-drive vehicle, and light aircraft in 1977.

I gained important background from Griffin Smith Jr., "Forgotten Places," (*Texas Monthly*, April 1977), 88-95.

I conducted pertinent interviews with John L. Guldemann, by telephone to Presidio County, Texas, 4 June 1991; Marion Tredaway, by telephone to Presidio County, circa 1982; and Julia Tredaway, by telephone to Presidio County, circa 1982.

The account of ghost bells in the Bofecillos is from Riley Aiken, "More Chisos Ghosts," as contained in Mody C. Boatright, Wilson M. Hudson, and Allen Maxwell, Editors, *Madstones and Twisters, Texas Folklore Society Publication No. 28* (Dallas: Southern Methodist University Press, 1958), 123-27.

Soloing the Guadalupes

This chapter is based solely on my backpack trek into the Guadalupe Mountains in April 1981.

Big Bend Adventurer

I based this account on my interviews with James Owens, Midland, Texas, January 1982, and 1983.

Comanche Springs Cave

I based this chapter partly on my own exploration of the cavern in September 1983.

I conducted the interview with Dennis Haynes, by telephone to Fort Stockton, Texas, in September 1983. The information regarding the cavern's rising water table in 1990 is from my interview with Mary Kay Shannon, Fort Stockton, 9 February 1990.

The notation that Comanche Springs ceased flowing in 1951 is from J. Evetts Haley, *Fort Concho and the Texas Frontier* (San Angelo: *San Angelo Standard-Times*, 1952), 3.

Mitre Peak's Might

I based this chapter largely on my series of climbs up Mitre Peak in 1978, 1979, 1981, and 1990. The "companion" mentioned in the text is Ben V. Ramon.

The tale of Mitre being the first place Satan touched Earth upon being cast out of Heaven is from Elton Miles, *Tales of the Big Bend* (College Station: Texas A&M Press, 1976), 20.

I conducted the interview with Dennis Nelson, by telephone to Alpine, Texas, in 1981.

The Girvin Site Dinosaur Tracks

I gained valuable background from Clint Kelley, "McCamey Group Hopes to Build Park Around Tracks of 'Big-Footed Mac'" (*The Midland Reporter-Telegram*, 27 December 1965); and June Luckett, "Culp Tracks Down an Ornithopod," unidentified and undated tearsheet in my possession.

I conducted pertinent interviews with Dr. Wann Langston, by telephone to Austin, Texas, February 1983 and 19 August 1991; and Jeff Pittman, by telephone to Beaumont, Texas, 19 August 1991 and 20 August 1991.

I gained background on *Acrocanthosaurus* from Paul Gregory, *Predatory Dinosaurs of the World* (New York: Simon and Shuster, 1988), 307-9, 311, 315; and Dr. David Norman, *The Illustrated Encyclopedia of Dinosaurs* (New York: Crescent Books, 1985), 67.

I also drew upon my personal investigation of the site.

Midland Man

For background, I consulted Fred Wendorf, Alex D. Krieger, and Claude C. Albritton, *The Midland Discovery: A Report on the Pleistocene Human Remains from Midland, Texas* (Austin: University of Texas Press, 1955).

I conducted pertinent interviews with Fred Wendorf, by telephone to Dallas, Texas, fall 1982 and 10 June 1991; Christy Turner, by telephone to Tempe, Arizona, fall 1982; Dee Ann Story, by telephone to Austin, Texas, fall 1982; Christopher Hill, by telephone to Dallas, 6 June 1991; and David Meltzer, Martin County, Texas, 20 June 1991.

The quote by Dr. Alex B. Krieger is from Anntoinette Moore, "'Midland Minnie' Star of County's Prehistoric Past Since 1953" (*Midland Reporter-Telegram*, 4 July 1985).

In a paper presented at the October 26, 1992 meeting of The Geological Society of America in Cincinnati, Ohio, Curtis R. McKinney reported that he had determined that Midland Man is about 11,600 years old. McKinney, director of geologic research at the Center for American Archeology in Kampsville, Illinois, used an improved technique called alpha spectrometry, which calculates age based on the ratio between thorium 230 and uranium 234. (Associated Press, "'Midland Woman' is the oldest American, geologist says," *Midland Reporter-Telegram*, 26 October 1992)

Mustang Springs

This chapter is based in part on my personal investigation of the site.

Information on the prehistory of Mustang Springs is from David J. Meltzer, whom I interviewed at the site on 20 June 1991. I also consulted Meltzer, "Altithermal Archaeology and Paleoecology at Mustang Springs, on the Southern High Plains of Texas," *American Antiquity*, 56(2), 1991, 236-37.

Information regarding Captain Randolph B. Marcy is from Marcy's journal as contained in Grant Foreman, *Marcy and the Gold Seekers* (Norman: University of Oklahoma Press, 2nd printing, 1968), 361-62.

Information regarding Lieutenant Nathaniel H. Michler is from *Reports of the Secretary of War*, 31st Congress, 1st Sess., Senate Executive Document No. 64 (Washington: 1850), 37.

Information regarding Brevet Captain John Pope is from Pope's log in House Executive Document No. 91, 33rd Congress, 2nd Sess., Vol. 2.

Information regarding Lieutenant Colonel William Shafter is from Shafter's report, as contained in "Shafter's Explorations in Western Texas, 1875," *West Texas Historical Association Year Book Vol. 9*, October 1933, 82-96.

The account of the last buffalo hunt is as told by Joe S. McCombs in Ben O. Grant and J. R. Webb, "On the Cattle Trail and Buffalo Range," *West Texas Historical Association Yearbook, Vol. 11*, November 1935, 100.

Camels, Ships of the Trans-Pecos

For background on the history of the camel corps, I drew upon George P. Marsh, *The Camel: His Organization Habits and Uses* (Boston: Gould and Lincoln, 1856); Chris Emmett, *Texas Camel Tales* (Austin: Steck-Vaughn Company, reprint 1969); Odie B. Faulk, *The U.S. Camel Corps: An Army Experiment* (New York: Oxford University Press, 1976); and Lewis Burt Lesley, Editor, *Uncle Sam's Camels: The Journal of May Humphreys Stacy* (Cambridge: Harvard University Press, 1929).

All information regarding the 1860 expedition of Brevet Second Lieutenant William H. Echols is from a typed transcript of Echols's log in my possession.

The account of the sighting of a camel in Million Dollar Canyon is from an interview with Richard Galle, Midland, Texas, 1989. Galle gained the account from the hikers, Lubbock, Texas, early 1970s.

Camp "Elizabeth"

For background history, I drew upon Ira Lee Watkins, "The History of Sterling County," as contained in Beverly Daniels, Editor, *Milling Around Sterling County* (Canyon: Staked Plains Press, Inc., 1976), 5-6, 9. Watkins cited early Sterling County pioneer W. F. Kellis as his source.

The account of the Indian fight involving Anglin is from "Record of Engagement with Hostile Indians in Texas 1868-1882," *West Texas Historical Association Year Book Vol. 9*, October 1933, 115; and from J. Evetts Haley, *Fort Concho and the Texas Frontier* (San Angelo: *San Angelo Standard-Times*, 1952), 327-28. Texas Ranger records give the date of the fight as 1 July 1879, whereas U.S. Army records give it as 30 June 1879. Information regarding Manning and Andy Jones is from Watkins, "The History of Sterling County." He cites W. F. Kellis as his source.

W. F. Kellis's comments regarding the graves are from the *Sterling City News-Record*, 15 January 1943. He indicates that the woman mentioned by George H. McEntire, Jr. died of tuberculosis, and that the adjoining grave is that of a boy, not a woman.

Kellis's comments regarding the North Concho River are from the *Sterling City News-Record*, 17 December 1943.

Measurements of the buildings are from "Camp Elizabeth," an unpublished paper written 13 December 1976 and on file at Fort Concho National Historic Landmark, San Angelo, Texas. Metric measurements were taken by Teddy and Francis Stickney of Midland Archeological Society and Shirley Pettengill of Concho Valley Archeological Society. Notes were taken by Shirley Pettengill. The paper indicates that the measurements are not to be taken as strictly accurate.

I conducted pertinent interviews with George H. McEntire, Jr., San Angelo, 15 July 1989; Ralph Davis, Sterling City, Texas, 4 March 1989 and 22 July 1989; J. Evetts Haley, by telephone to Midland, Texas, 5 February 1990; and John Neilson, by telephone to San Angelo, 8 August 1991.

I also drew upon my personal investigation of the camp ruins, soldiers' graves, and buffalo hunters' defense pit in September 1991 and on other occasions.

Derricks and Gushers

I interviewed W. W. "Bill" Allman in Crane, Texas, in spring 1983. He died 21 April 1990.

Information regarding Ben Wray's sparring session with Jack Dempsey comes from Randy Roberts, *Jack Dempsey, the Manassa Mauler* (Baton Rouge: Louisiana State University Press, 1979), 155. P. O. "Slim" Vines remembered Wray as still "kind

Notes on Sources

of crooked-jawed" when they both worked for Gulf in the 1930s. Vines's comment came in an interview with me in Crane, Texas, 16 August 1989.

Boxcars and Brakies

This account is based on my freight train ride from Big Spring, Texas, to Monahans, Texas, and on my simultaneous interviews with the principals in March 1982.

Hoboes

I based this narrative entirely on my experiences in the Odessa, Texas, freight yards in June 1981.

Hobo Bill

I interviewed Wild Bill and The Quiet One in the Odessa, Texas, freight yards in June 1981.

The Border

This account is based entirely on my ride with the Border Patrol, Del Rio Sector, and my simultaneous interviews with the principals, circa 1984.

In the Border Patrol "Game"

This account is based entirely on my ride with the Border Patrol in Midland, Texas, and my simultaneous interviews with the principals, circa 1986.

The I-1-5-1 legal resident alien card has since been updated.

A law making employers subject to administrative fines if they knowingly hire illegal aliens went into effect in 1986. Bill Holman, assistant chief patrol agent for the U.S. Border Patrol Marfa Sector, noted in an interview with me on 19 August 1991 that Marfa Sector agents have apprehended somewhat fewer illegal aliens since that time. He added, however, that "we still have the [same] percentage ... [of] repeaters coming back."

The Illegal Women

I based this chapter on my interview with Elfida and Irma in Midland, Texas, circa 1986.

Notes on Sources

An Alien Struggle

I interviewed Ricardo in Glasscock County, Texas, with the aid of Billy Torres, interpreter, circa 1984.

Lariat and Hot Iron

This account is based entirely on my observation of branding on the Scharbauer Brothers and Company's Crowley Ranch, Midland County, Texas, in February 1982.

The Last Cowboy

This account is based partly on my investigation and interviews at the site of the ongoing manhunt, Coke County, Texas, 3 June 1976. I also hiked the area extensively in June 1990 and on other occasions.

I conducted pertinent interviews with Fred McCabe, Sr., Coke County, 3 June 1976; Paul Burns, Coke County, 3 June 1976, and by telephone to Robert Lee, Texas, 4 August 1991; Wayne McCabe, Coke County, 3 June 1976, and by telephone to Robert Lee, 3 August 1991; Roy Ivey, San Angelo, Texas, 4 June 1976; Melvin Childress, by telephone to Robert Lee, 4 June 1976; J. Lee Ensor, Coke County, 3 June 1976, and by telephone to Bronte, Texas, 3 August 1991; the unnamed former inmate, by telephone to San Angelo, 4 June 1976; Marshall Millican, by telephone to Coke County, 5 June 1976, and by telephone to Robert Lee, 5 August 1991; Arthur Sikes, by telephone to San Angelo, 7 August 1991; James Allen, by telephone to Brownwood, Texas, 4 August 1991; Ernest Haynes, by telephone to San Angelo, 5 August 1991; Helen Mathers, by telephone to Robert Lee, 4 August 1991; Joy Spradlin, by telephone to Grand Prairie, Texas, 7 August 1991 and 10 August 1991; and David Young, Texas Department of Corrections public relations official, by telephone to Austin, Texas, 8 August 1991.

Quotes attributed to Mrs. Walter Douglas Cook of Sabinal, Texas, are from a letter written by Mrs. Cook, June 1976.

Charles Walls's description and information on his early life, schooling, and marriage are from Mrs. Spradlin, who, along with Mrs. Cook, noted his U.S. Navy stint.

Childress detailed Walls's preference to go bearded, while Millican and Mrs. Cook noted his western attire and Mrs. Cook and Sikes described his boots.

Description of his tattoos is from Mrs. Cook.

Information on his name is from Mrs. Spradlin, Mrs. Cook, Wayne McCabe, Sikes, Millican, Ensor, and Haynes.

Information relating to Walls's alcohol use comes from Childress, the unnamed inmate, Wayne McCabe, and Mrs. Spradlin.

The notation of his rodeo days is from the unnamed inmate and Ensor. Walls was never a member of the Professional Rodeo Cowboys Association, according to PRCA records at Prorodeo Hall of Fame, Colorado Springs, Colorado.

Details of Walls's conviction for burglary come from Fifty-first District records, supplied by Sharon Lee of the district clerk's office, Coke County Courthouse, Robert Lee, 12 August 1991.

Information about Walls driving a cattle truck comes from Millican, who, along with Childress, noted his work as a ranch hand.

Details of the jeep theft, as well as of Walls's arrest, conviction, and sentencing for the third degree felony, are from Fifty-first District Court Records in Tom Green County Courthouse, San Angelo.

An official with the district attorney's office in San Angelo supplied details of the high-speed pursuit in an oral statement to me, circa 1976.

Incarceration dates are from Young.

Sikes supplied information on the taking of the tractor and horse, while Wayne McCabe related additional details on the latter theft in a 22 August 1991 letter to me.

Information about the Ray Stewart Ranch comes from Burns and Wayne McCabe.

Information regarding the warrant at the time of the manhunt is from Carol Finney O'Neil, "Manhunt/Coke County suspect on horseback sought," *San Angelo Standard-Times*, evening edition, 3 June 1976.

For information relating to Walls's death and subsequent examination of the body (including quotes from Gene Dupertuis, or Depertuis), I drew upon William D. Kerns, "'Cowboy' Walls Killed Sunday in California," *San Angelo Standard-Times* 19 June 1976. Sikes supplied additional details, both in the interview and in a letter to me 15 August 1991.

Index

꿍